THE BOOK OF
MANIFESTATIONS

Designed by Ashley Millhouse
Type set in Gill Sans MT Condensed/Chronicle Text

ISBN: 978-0-7643-5971-2
Printed in China

Published by Red Feather Mind, Body, Spirit
An imprint of Schiffer Publishing, Ltd.
4880 Lower Valley Road
Atglen, PA 19310
Phone: (610) 593-1777; Fax: (610) 593-2002
E-mail: Info@schifferbooks.com
Web: www.redfeathermbs.com

For our complete selection of fine books on this and related subjects, please visit our website at www.schifferbooks.com. You may also write for a free catalog.

Schiffer Publishing's titles are available at special discounts for bulk purchases for sales promotions or premiums. Special editions, including personalized covers, corporate imprints, and excerpts, can be created in large quantities for special needs. For more information, contact the publisher.

We are always looking for people to write books on new and related subjects. If you have an idea for a book, please contact us at proposals@schifferbooks.com.

THE BOOK OF
MANIFESTATIONS

Practical Ways to Attract Your Deepest Desires

MISHAL

REDFeather™
MIND | BODY | SPIRIT

4880 Lower Valley Road, Atglen, PA 19310

WELCOME

The most powerful law of the Universe is what brought you here.

A part of you wanted to do much more with life and made you pick up this book. A part of me *also* wanted to do much more with life and urged me to type my insights for you to read. The *Law of Attraction* (LOA) is what brought the both of us together.

Like attracts like—that's the simple essence of a law that pervades *everything* we can think of. Similar particles coalesce to become stars and planets, like-minded individuals converge to the same cities, people with identical interests form clubs and social circles, and lovers with similar personalities tend have long-lasting unions. Birds of a feather *always* flock together.

But despite the Law's obvious nature, most people are unable to harness its power to their advantage because they simply do not know *how to*. Most are unaware of the *simple* things that can be done on a daily basis to ensure that the Universe has no option but to bring their desires right to them.

This book contains thirty practical processes that make use of the powerful and all-encompassing Law of Attraction—processes that will help you make giant strides toward the life you'd prefer to be living.

Throughout the book, special efforts have been made to remove the abstractness from the Law and make it as "user-friendly" as possible. Each chapter explains a process and then encourages you to fit it into your everyday life with the help of the eye-opening exercises that follow. It's only when you've added your *own touch* to the ideas being offered that you will be able to harness this Law to powerful effect and make your life what it was meant to be.

While prior knowledge of the Law of Attraction is assumed, even those new to the concept will benefit immensely from the ideas mentioned. After all, we could all do with any sort of information that makes our lives better, right? And there isn't a better place to start than by educating yourself on the finer aspects of an "idea" that has rightfully captured the public's imagination since the past two decades.

Truth be told, the Law of Attraction is all that there is. And in a world that can easily overwhelm, it's imperative that we make use of this all-powerful and all-encompassing law to supplement our efforts and, most importantly, bring the joy back into our lives.

That's exactly what this book will help you do.

CONTENTS

CHAPTER ONE

LEVERAGE THE SMALL STUFF

The higher you vibrate, the faster you will be able to manifest the things you desire. It is law.

By vibration, I mean the general life force flowing through and to you; it's how much energy you possess. If that still doesn't make sense, it's how happy and enthusiastic you are in this red-hot moment.

The more *alive* you feel, the more the Universe will present itself to you and give you fantastic insights on how to get to your desires, making you feel even more energized. The more *lifeless* you feel, the more the Universe will turn its back on you. That's just how this whole game works.

You cannot act like a zombie and expect the good things to pop into your life; that would defy the most powerful law of the universe—the Law of Attraction. When you are not a *vibrational match* to happiness, circumstances that make you happy cannot come into your experience. Happiness breeds more happiness, and sadness leads to circumstances that make us feel *even more* miserable.

The *only* reason we have ended up becoming zombies and have self-manufactured a great deal of sadness in our lives is because we have made our happiness *conditional* on lovers / jobs / houses / cars / vacation destinations / perfect health. The unavailability of our desires bothers us, which prevents them from happening, which bothers us even more, which pushes them further away—a vicious spiral.

The best way, then, to get the joy back into your life, break away from a downward spiral, and live the amazing life that you were meant to be living is by placing your happiness in the small things in life—the ones *always* within your grasp.

When you consciously make it a point to enjoy the small things you have easy access to—like listening to uplifting music, taking a walk in the park, making a great cup of hot chocolate for yourself, watching a funny movie, reading your favorite book, gazing at the stars, meditating, cycling downhill, cooking your favorite dish, petting your dog, installing a fish tank, planting flowers in your garden, going for long drives, or lighting fireworks in the night sky—your vibration will automatically rise.

Once your vibration has risen, you will attain the *energy currency* that will help in manifesting the bigger stuff. This energy currency is all that you will ever need (money, ultimately, being a form of energy in itself) to get everything you want.

So, if you want to feel rich and alive all the time, keep your focus on the small things, always; these everyday moments must form the core of your happy life. The small joys of life will never turn their back on you or demand that you behave differently for them to be available for you. The bigger events may come and go, but the small ones will stick around and help you manifest the "larger" stuff.

Enjoy the small things that give you happiness, soak in the feelings that they elicit from you, and, most of all, appreciate their energetic value and consistency.

So, start this journey by **making a comprehensive list of the small things that make you happy,** and using the activities within this list to raise your vibration as often as you can.

And always keep the small stuff in your life on priority, even when everything else seems to be going very well.

Small things that make me happy

CHAPTER TWO

TRUST YOUR INNER GPS

The infinite intelligence within us knows the fastest, easiest, and most scenic route to where we want to go, and is constantly giving us directions to get there.

That little voice inside us that we call our *intuition* is actually like a sophisticated GPS system that not only knows where we are right now, but also where we ought to be heading in every moment of our lives to reach our desired destination.

Our *inner GPS* knows which streets are empty, when the lines at the grocery store are short, the food that will do wonders to our health, the book that will change our life, the job that is best suited for our personality, and the partner who will keep us happy in the long run; it knows everything!

So advanced is this system that if we only knew how to follow the directions it keeps giving us, we would always stay on track to where we want to go, and our lives would feel like a dream filled with joy, freedom, purpose, and direction.

The only reason we have been led astray from the joyful path that we were meant to be living is because this GPS sound has been *drowned out* by the loud music being played around us in the form of external influences. That is, we have ended up listening to others more than we have been listening to ourselves.

It is not uncommon for most of us to receive a bombardment of advice from all fronts these days—advice from people who care for us but don't have the slightest clue about our inner desires and wants. But the more we listen to this loud music, the less we are able to hear our inner GPS, and we eventually end up going somewhere we never wanted to go to in the first place.

So, the next time you think a thought or want to do something, ask yourself if this thought came from "inside" or "outside." Almost every time, an outside thought will lead to frustration in the end.

Listen to yourself, make your own mistakes, carve your own path, make spontaneous decisions, plan less and play more, think from your belly and not your brain, and learn to follow your bliss. If something doesn't feel blissful in the moment, you probably shouldn't be doing it.

Your own decisions may or may not lead to immediate success, but you will always be happy doing them. This happiness will give you the energy to pursue even more fun activities, and the spiral will continue upward.

Muster the courage to stick to your own decisions, even in the face of opposition from the world around you. Only if you are true to yourself will you find true wealth—

not only in terms of money in the bank, but also through the improved quality of your relationships, a general sense of freedom, and that lovely feeling of immense joy.

Meditation is a great way to hear this subtle GPS voice more clearly. At first, because there are so many thoughts in your head, you'll find it hard to distinguish between the ones that are truly your own and those that have been planted into your consciousness by society, but as you meditate and quiet your mind, you'll find it easier and easier to distinguish between the two.

The thought that seemingly comes out of "nowhere" is your inner GPS telling you what to do. The thoughts that are constantly going on in the background, like a radio, are the ones that won't help you when you have to make major life decisions.

Learn to trust the guidance that comes from within and do not be afraid to make mistakes; even if you take a wrong turn today, your GPS will always redirect you to your destination. Just make sure you mute or lower the outside music when you reach a critical turn in your life.

Identifying the loud music

List three people who give you the most advice:		
The person you get most advice from:	Has this person achieved success in the area of your life he/she is giving you advice on? (Yes/No)	Is the life they have lived, or are living, something you'd like to emulate? (Yes/No)
1		
2		
3		

Turning up the sound of your GPS

What time of the day are you most likely to be by yourself?		
Time of the day	Are you by yourself?	What activities could you do at this time to hear your inner voice clearly? (Meditate, journal, spend time in absolute silence, go for a walk without your phone, clear out clutter, offer help to people unknown to you, etc.)
6–8 AM		
8–10 AM		
10–12 noon		
2–4 PM		
4–6 PM		
6–8 PM		
8–10 PM		
10–12 midnight		
12–2 AM		
2–4 AM		
4–6 AM		

CHAPTER THREE

GET CLOSE TO NATURE

There is something inexplicably healing, refreshing, energizing, and stimulating about nature that does wonders for the mind, body, and spirit.

Mother Nature's presence unfailingly soothes us into a state of mind that increases our vibration, allows us to think high-quality thoughts, and makes us much more optimistic about what lies ahead.

So drastic are the consequences of being disconnected from our true habitat that close to half the problems we experience today are because we are not living the way nature had intended for us to live.

We human beings are physically designed to be out and about this planet's natural surroundings, not resigned to be sitting behind a desk or imprisoned inside our houses for the best part of our lives. People who live close to nature have far more peaceful, enjoyable, and healthier lives than the ones perennially stuck in the hustle-bustle of the city.

So, for the sake of your own mental and physical health, take a step back and make it a priority to bask in nature, as often as you can. Make the park next to your house your second home and notice how the problems in your life reduce. Go for long walks, sunbathe, make a trip to the nearest beach, trek a mountain, go boating in a lake, gaze at the night sky, feed the birds, or take a walk in the woods; it will make you realize how petty some of your worries are.

If you can't make the time to go out into nature on a regular basis, then bring a bit of nature *into* your home. Increase the size of your windows so more air and sunlight can make their way in, place small plants on the grills of your window or at the corners of your house, purchase flowers on the weekend and put them in a vase on your dining table, buy a fish tank for the lobby of your building, put a bird feeder at your window, and if you are feeling really opulent, install a water fountain somewhere you can see it often. These activities will always improve the energies of your house.

We are all receptive to the energies around us; it's this inherent quality of ours that allows us to benefit and soak in the goodness of nature. This receptivity is what makes us feel good when are out where we belong, doing the things that nature has designed us to do, and soaking in some of the highest energies we have access to.

It always makes sense to be out in the open, because the vibration of nature is higher than anything else that we can ever imagine. How else could you explain its perennial existence, without anything to ever feed it? The sun has been shining for billions of years and will continue to do so for at least a few billion years more, the clouds have been pouring rain since soon after this planet was formed, rivers have been flowing since before the evolution of humans, and Earth's soil has continually given us crop after crop after crop.

All the material riches of the world pale in comparison with the richness of nature. We are just so used to thinking of abundance in terms of money in the bank that we have forgotten that you cannot put a price on sunshine, the oxygen in the air, the pouring of rain, the existence of trees, or the singing of birds.

Can you imagine what our expenses would be if the sun, clouds, rivers, and crops demanded money for going about their business, like we humans do? We'd all go broke in no time.

So, **learn to appreciate and make full use of all the free stuff in life**, and watch how the material riches follow. It is law.

How close are you and Mother Nature?

List ten places within a hundred mile radius of your house that you consider to be close to nature. (Park, beach, lake, resort, holiday home, waterfall, zoo, hiking camp, etc.)

	Places you consider close to nature:	Number of times you've been there in the past 12 months (0, 1– 4, 5 –10, 10+)
1		
2		
3		
4		
5		
6		
7		
8		
9		
10		

Getting out

List the number of times you have performed the following activities in the past twelve months. (0, 1– 4, 5–10, 10+)	
Watched the sunrise	
Watched the sunset	
Gazed at the full moon	
Consciously stood in sunlight for a while	
Watered a plant	
Fed an animal	
Cooked a full meal for yourself	
Gone for a walk outdoors, without your phone	
Taken a bath with cold water	
Engaged in some form of outdoor recreation (outdoor sports, paintball, skiing, hiking, boating, paragliding, sailing, watersports, etc.)	
See the Appendix for how these activities have a direct impact on some of the things you'd like to manifest.	

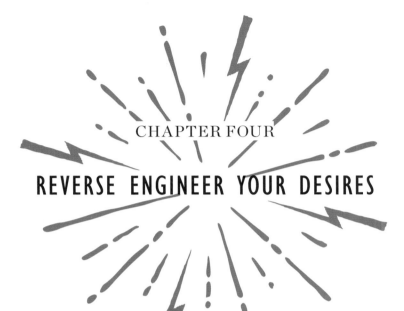

CHAPTER FOUR

REVERSE ENGINEER YOUR DESIRES

The number one reason you want to manifest anything in your life (drum roll, please) is because of how you'd *feel* in the having of it.

Go ahead; think of anything that you desire, and notice the emotion you'd feel upon the accomplishment of this desire. The car, the boyfriend or girlfriend, the house, the chiseled body, the lovemaking, the vacation, or just about anything under the sun; if you want it, it's because you will feel a certain positive emotion such as *pride, security, bliss, satisfaction, power,* or *excitement* when you finally get it.

The catch, however, is that you have to feel it to get it.

Think of manifestation as a *feeling game.* The more you are feeling good about your desire, the closer you are to it. The more you are feeling bad about not having this desire, the more it is running away from you. It's really as simple as that.

So, to get what your desire, learn to keep the *emotion* behind it at a priority, not the actual desire itself. Your desire will have no option but to make its way to you once you start feeling the emotion associated with the desire, on a regular basis.

Let me explain how this works. First, identify the exact emotion behind your desire; picture yourself having already accomplished what you've been wanting, and the *feelings* it would conjure up inside you. Go ahead, take a few minutes and visualize yourself actually living this desire. Imagine it in your hands; imagine it engaging all your senses; imagine yourself experiencing all of it, right here and right now.

How do you feel in the having of it? Of course, you are feeling happy, but can you get more specific about how you are *feeling*? Are you feeling *confident, secure, proud, excited, satisfied, gratified, powerful, relieved, ecstatic,* or just *blissful*? Take a minute to identify the emotion.

Once you have figured out the actual emotion behind your desire, *start chasing this emotion on a moment-to-moment basis.* If the job you want is because it will make you feel proud of yourself, start chasing that emotion. The right job *has to* come your way when you are vibrating pride.

One of the best ways of rapidly getting on the frequency of pride is by asking yourself the magic question: *What can I do right now that will make me feel slightly more proud of myself?* Then follow the impulse that comes as often as you can during the day.

The impulse could lead you to open a Word document so you can start typing in your CV; it could make you want to get a haircut, so you start looking more presentable, or it could just make you want to get out your house for some exercise. There are several things you could do *in the moment* that would make you feel *slightly more proud* of yourself, putting you on the right energetic track to get what you are after.

By chasing the emotion of your manifestation on a moment-to-moment basis, reverse engineering will help you get on the frequency of your desire, causing it to rapidly manifest into your experience. All the *tiny* steps that you consciously take will go a long way in helping you get what you are after.

Each manifestation carries with it an accompanying emotion; always chase that particular emotion if you want the manifestation to occur faster. If you want someone to date, chase excitement and anticipation, not the lover. If you want to win a trophy or a competition, chase pride. If you want to rise up the ranks in your organization, chase the feelings of power. If you want a perfectly healthy body, chase the feelings of confidence.

You will be surprised with how beautifully and quickly the Law of Attraction will start lining up circumstances that make you feel ever-increasing amounts of the emotion that you are after, once you start chasing it on a moment-to-moment basis.

Not only will this moment-to-moment orientation keep you motivated, since you will be continually breaking down your ultimate energetic goal into much-smaller goals, but it will also give you the incentive to take action because the enormity of the task ahead won't feel so daunting anymore.

Reverse engineering is one of those rare processes that will allow you to live and enjoy the present moment and at the same time propel you toward your long-term goals.

Identifying the emotion

List ten things you desire the most, and the emotion you would feel when you get them.

	Desire	The emotion at the point of manifestation
1		
2		
3		
4		
5		
6		
7		
8		
9		
10		

Reverse engineering your #1 Desire

	Activities you could do on a regular basis to *feel* the emotion behind this desire
1	
2	
3	
4	
5	
6	
7	
8	
9	
10	

CHAPTER FIVE

MAKE USE OF THE 80/20 PRINCIPLE

Probably one of the most powerful, yet unknown, phenomenon in the world—the rule of 80/20—was first studied in 1906 by Italian economist Vilfredo Pareto when he noticed that 20 percent of the pea pods in his garden were responsible for producing 80 percent of the peas in it—an observation that struck him as unusual.

Pareto decided to test this bizarre finding in his preferred subject of macroeconomics, and there, too, he found that 20 percent of the people in Italy owned 80 percent of the wealth of the country—adding credibility to his earlier finding, which suggested unequal distribution among observable phenomena.

Several successful and diverse tests later, he went on to create a mathematical formula to describe this strange distribution of wealth (among other things) in his country, which came to be known as the Pareto principle or the "80/20 rule."

The crux of this rule is that *matter and energy are always going to be distributed in a lopsided manner* in a way that almost seems unfair. Very rarely will one find an equal, or a 50/50 distribution, in anything that surrounds them. A few of the many ways in which this principle expresses itself in our existence are listed below.

- Of all the heavenly bodies in our solar system, all known life is found only in one; a planet with only a tiny fraction of the landmass of the entire system, yet harboring 100 percent of its life.
- Out of the 200 odd countries on this planet, the richest ten account for more than 80 percent of the gross domestic product (GDP) and wealth.
- In most nations, more than 80 percent of the population is found in 20 percent or less of the area within it (with the majority staying in the major cities).
- In cities, 80 percent of the traffic is usually out during 20 percent of the day (peak office-going hours).
- In any office, 80 percent of the work usually takes place during 20 percent of the workday (with the rest wasted under the pretense of being busy or in idle chitchat).
- And while an employee is idling away, 80 percent or more of his or her social interactions occur with fewer than 20 percent of the colleagues in the office (the ones she is most comfortable talking to).

The 80/20 rule, or inequality in general, is present everywhere in the world—and in everything that you do. **Make serious attempts to spot the 80/20 phenomenon in your life, and use it to your advantage.**

Structure your life in such a way that you maximize the time you spend on the *few* activities and people that are resulting in 80 percent of your happiness, and minimize the time you spend on the ones that are causing 80 percent of your unhappiness.

Spend more time with the 20 percent people in your life that are making you feel 80 percent of the love that you experience; spend less time with the 20 percent who ignite strong negative emotions within you. Visit 20 percent of the places that make you feel blissful, and avoid the ones that make you wish you were someplace else. Do 20 percent of those activities that make you feel alive and in the moment, and reduce your time on the ones that suck away your energy.

Become obsessive when it comes to doing the things that make you happy. If relaxing by the swimming pool helps you unwind like nothing else does, do not hesitate in going there whenever you have time to spare. If listening to a song that was just released is making you forget your problems, play it on repeat until you squeeze all the juice out of it. If eating a particular dish is making you love your life, cook it as often as you can, until you tire of it, and then find your next favorite dish.

Once you start leveraging the power of the 80/20 principle in your life, you, too, will be among the top 20 percent of the happiest/successful/energetic people in your social circle, and the spiral will only continue upward.

Expanding the best 20%

20% of the activities in your life that result in 80% of the happiness that you experience:

20% of the people causing 80% of your happiness:

20% of the places giving you your 80% happiness:

Minimizing the worst 20%

20% of the activities resulting in 80% of the unhappiness that you experience:

20% of the people causing 80% of your unhappiness:

20% of the places that result in 80% of your stress:

CHAPTER SIX

BREAK DOWN THE BARRIERS

The only reason you aren't getting what you want is because a part of you doesn't want to experience it right now, period!

There are subconscious blocks within you that are holding you apart from your own desires. Blocks so powerful that no matter how much you consciously desire something, they have the ability to prevent it from happening.

Our conscious mind may want something to happen and could even be *desperate* for it, but if there are subconscious blocks to this desire, then there is a tug of war that takes place between the conscious and the subconscious mind, which kills us from inside. There's more bad news: The subconscious mind almost always wins—leaving us feeling frustrated and helpless.

One of the best ways, then, of figuring out and overcoming the self-created blocks to your desires, and luring the subconscious on the side of the conscious mind, is by asking yourself this: Why do I *not* want this particular desire right now? That is, try to **figure out what is it about your desire that you do not want, and aim to cancel that out.**

So, if you're single and consciously want to get into a relationship but haven't been able to manifest a lover despite your best efforts, ask yourself *why you do not want a boyfriend/girlfriend right now*.

You may not want a lover because you are afraid he might break your heart, or you may be embarrassed about your house and not want to bring someone home; you could be conscious of your weight or feel that getting into a relationship would take your focus away from work—the reasons could be many. Just make a note of them.

After you've figured out the reasons you do *not* want your desire, aim to cancel the top three out with appropriate actions and affirmations.

If you do not want a boyfriend because you are afraid that he might break your heart, make yourself as independent and self-sufficient as possible, so your happiness does not depend on anyone else. Engage in extracurricular activities that give you a sense of direction and purpose outside your work, help you make friends, keep you occupied, and make you realize that there is more to life than just being in a relationship; so, even if your future lover were to break your heart, you'd have plenty of friends and activities to fall back on for support. And while you are doing this, affirm that "I am an independent man/woman who knows how to take care of myself, and my happiness depends *only* on me" for two minutes before you sleep.

If you are feeling embarrassed of your house and fret about bringing someone home, start taking care of your house in a way that makes it seem inviting and presentable to anyone who would enter for the first time. Pick up any good feng shui book and practice the art, make serious efforts to clean things up, employ someone to help you with your housework, and start giving your house the respect it deserves. The affirmation for this could be something on the lines of "My house is an extension of the lovely human being that I am. I do my best to take care of it."

If weight is an issue, join a gym, track your steps with a pedometer, watch your diet, take the stairs instead of the elevator, drink green tea twice a day, and buy clothes that complement your body type. And you can affirm that "Every day and in every way, I grow fitter and fitter" before you sleep.

Your actions and affirmations will go a long way in canceling out the powerful blocks that are preventing your desires from manifesting.

Avoid trying to *force* the manifestation that you desire, by doing things like going out to bars in the hope of finding someone, uploading your profile on dating apps, or just about anything else, until you have made efforts to cancel out your blocks. Even if you find someone before the blocks have been canceled out, the relationship won't give you the happiness you expect, and probably won't last long either. Cancel out the blocks and then the lover will *come to you*, even without much effort on your part.

When your barriers to a particular desire are removed/reduced, and the subconscious and conscious minds are working in tandem, your desire will manifest very quickly.

It's only because of these subconscious barriers that our manifestations are being held apart from us. We all are too powerful, too worthy, and too deserving for any person, economy, or "mysterious force" to be able to prevent us from attaining the things we want. We are getting in our own way!

Identifying and breaking down the barriers

Write down something you desire that hasn't manifested yet.		

Now, let's tackle the blocks:

Blocks (Why do you NOT want this desire to manifest right now?)	Appropriate Actions (What can you do to cancel out this block?)	Affirmation (What can you say out loud to gradually break down this subconscious barrier?)

Identifying and breaking down the barriers (II)

What else do you desire, right now? (This could even be a block from the previous exercise, preventing you from attaining your #1 desire.)

Block(s)	Appropriate Action(s)	Affirmation

CHAPTER SEVEN

ANCHOR YOUR DAY

One of the biggest barriers that gets in the way of our desires is our subconscious resistance to any sort of *change*.

Most of us love the status quo, because whenever we encounter change, our conscious mind typically goes into overdrive to assess its impact on our life—to gauge whether this new place/person/circumstance is good for us, or if it offers a threat in some way. And since the mind is always trying to save energy, we subconsciously end up resisting all change (even the good type).

Resistance to change is why so many prefer to stick to the jobs they've been doing for a while, even though there might be better opportunities elsewhere. It's why we prefer to spend time with old and known friends. It's why many people stick to the towns they grew up in for their entire lives. And it's why some continue to be in abusive relationships because of their irrational fear of the uncertainty that would accompany the ending of the relationship.

All human beings have an aversion toward uncertainty; not knowing what lies ahead can drive some of us crazy and make us do things that are counterproductive. Yet, acceptance of uncertainty is vital for us to become receptive to all that we've been asking for. In fact, *any manifestation requires a change from the status quo* and an acceptance of the uncertainty that comes with it. If it weren't for change, we'd always get what we already have, and our desires would *never* come to us.

One of the best ways, then, of becoming more open to change in a way that allows all those lovely manifestations in is through a process called *anchoring*. This is a technique that involves you forming a *constant* in your life, by doing any one activity of your choice, at the same time every day, for the rest of your life!

That is, if you wish to anchor your day and your life, **do absolutely anything you like; just make sure you do it at the same time, every single day.**

So, if you like going for a run in the morning, start doing that every day, at the same time, and don't miss a single day. If you find running too demanding to be done every day, then you can even do something small like drinking green tea at the same time every day. It doesn't even have to be something healthy; even if you want to watch reruns of *Friends* and eat nachos with cheese while doing so, do it at the same time, every day! Just make sure this is an activity that you'd want to do for the rest of your life.

Anchoring your day with something that you are fond of doing will go a long way in reducing any barriers to change. You will now have a deep and subconscious understanding that no matter how much your life changes, *there will always be something that remains the same,* and this is what will make you more open toward accepting improvements in your life that may require a departure from what you consider to be familiar territory.

When you choose an activity for this process, make sure it's something that you'd be able to do even when you are traveling or out of town. *Choose absolutely anything for any number of minutes; just stick with it, no matter what.* (Even drinking a glass of water at the same time will do wonders.)

You'll begin to notice the power of this process within a few days of practicing it. And in the long run, anchoring will make you more open to moving out of your comfort zone, meeting new people, and trying new activities, and more willing to let go of the things/people that aren't serving you. All those lovely desires won't feel alien anymore, as this process will help you strike a delicious balance between self-created certainty (in the form of this Anchored Activity) and the uncertainty that is the very nature of our existence and expansion.

It's really a wonderful feeling to be able to give yourself a sense of *security and certainty* in this ever-changing world. Anchoring will help you do that and much more.

Choosing your anchor

Write down ten things you love doing:			
Activity	Is it easy and convenient to do?	Can it be done independently?	Would you want to do this for the rest of your life?
1			
2			
3			
4			
5			
6			
7			
8			
9			
10			

Zeroing in on the time

Time Period	Are you answerable to someone?	Are you by yourself?
00:00–02:00		
02:00–04:00		
04:00–06:00		
06:00–08:00		
08:00–10:00		
10:00–12:00		
12:00–14:00		
16:00–18:00		
18:00–20:00		
20:00–22:00		
22:00–24:00		

CHAPTER EIGHT

APPLY THE 24-HOUR TECHNIQUE

Our subconscious mind cannot differentiate between what's real and what's being imagined. Use this loophole to your full advantage by *pretending* to live the kind of life the best version of you would be living in the future, and your subconscious will have no option but to respond and bring this dream life to you.

Visualize yourself living the best possible life you can imagine in the near future, and pay attention to the *time of the day* you would be waking up, exercising, taking a shower, having your breakfast, going to work, socializing, relaxing at home, and going to bed. Pay attention to your fantastic future wristwatch while doing this visualization (Rolex, anyone?), and keep glancing at it after you complete the activities described above.

And from now on, make an attempt to follow this schedule as much as you possibly can. Start by setting the alarm clock to the time your future self is waking up (and give him or her an imaginary high five when you *do* get up at that time).

Once you've gotten your waking time set in your daily schedule, proceed toward the other activities. Start having your breakfast at the same time as your future self, and then start exercising at the same time, slowly taking this momentum toward all the other activities.

The reason that *time* is so important in this exercise, and the previous one, is because it's the one thing that remains constant and unchanging in our physical experience. Everything else in our life—the friends we hang out with, our beliefs and attitudes, the money in our bank accounts, what we do for a living, who we are deeply in love with—will change, but the way we experience time will always remain the same.

And the point of this process is to make use of the constant nature of time and to live the life your future self is living. **The more you mimic your future self's schedule, the faster you will get to where he or she is**, eventually reaching a point where your daily schedule looks exactly like your best self.

Places can also be very interesting when it comes to this exercise. If you know where your future self is staying, try visiting that place as often as you can. He or she will obviously be going for walks close to that area, so go for a walk there every once in a while.

If you know which places your future self goes for recreation, go to those places as well. Which places does he or she go to watch movies? Which place does he or she get a haircut? Which places does he or she play sports? Which gym does he or she go to?

What does his or her physique look like? Which places does he or she go to eat? What kind of people does he or she hang out with? Keep all this in mind and visit those places whenever you get the time.

Play around with this technique a lot more than you would with anchoring; try walking the way your future self would walk, try talking to people the way your future self would talk, and try being as confident as your future self. You'll notice that you will form a deep bond with yourself once you start doing this exercise.

The aim should be to experience the 24 hours in the day the way your future self is experiencing it. The smaller the gap between your future self's schedule and yours, the faster the process will work.

They say there is a parallel version of you *already* living the life of your dreams; it's the reason you currently have the desires that have already been experienced by you in the future. Your job is to merge into that reality.

Once you form a bond with your future self by giving him or her company, he or she will give you insights on what needs to be done to get to where he or she is.

Describe an ideal weekday for your future-self

Time	Activity	Notes
00:00–02:00		
02:00–04:00		
04:00–06:00		
06:00–08:00		
08:00–10:00		
10:00–12:00		
12:00–14:00		
14:00–16:00		
16:00–18:00		
18:00–20:00		
20:00–22:00		
22:00–00:00		

Where is your future-self spending most of his/her time?

Activity	Place where this is occuring
Residing	
Going for a walk	
Working out	
Going for a haircut	
Watching movies	
Playing outdoor sports	
Dining out	
Vacationing	
Going for a drive	
Getting the car repaired	
Getting a massage	
Relaxing or lounging around	
Praying/meditating	
Working	

CHAPTER NINE

TAME THE MONKEY MIND

The most wonderful and complex object in the known universe is that delicate piece of tissue inside our head that we call our brain. A relatively small organ that has the largest impact on the quality of our life, and the happiness (or the lack of it) that we experience on a daily basis—and the power of which, *if harnessed*, has the ability to give us everything we desire.

Most are not aware of this, but almost every circumstance of ours has been conjured up by the mind either on a conscious or a subconscious level. And at every moment, either the mind controls us by making us worried, stressed, or anxious, or we control our mind by thinking about the things we would *love* to experience—thereby bringing them closer to us.

So, it's really up to you to learn to control your mind and not allow it to wreak havoc on your existence by letting it do whatever it wants to. A certain amount of mental discipline to think thoughts of positivity is needed to make it through life, let alone thrive.

Thinking about the things you would like to experience brings them closer to you, and thinking about the things you *do not* want to experience *also* brings them closer to you; that's just how the Law of Attraction works. So, to master the Law, you have to learn to be selective about what you give your attention to, and know how to take your attention away from what isn't working in your life.

One of the hardest skills to master is learning to be selective about your focus. It can be especially difficult if you have problems such as being overdue on your debt payments, out of a job, in the middle of a messy divorce, or down with a disease. In fact, it can be close to impossible to not think about something that has turned your life upside down.

And here's where you must learn to use the power of *distraction* to your benefit. What would you do to a monkey that is creating havoc in your house? Most people would have no idea what to do and panic, hoping it would somehow find its own way out. Others would try to aggressively push it out, causing it to do further damage. But the right approach would be to distract the monkey with bananas or peanuts, calm him down, and eventually lure him out of the premises.

That's exactly what you have to do to your mind when it is thinking about the things you do not want—**distract it with activities that will calm it down**—like exercising rigorously, meeting friends and talking about fun stuff, watching an engrossing movie, playing a sport with someone who is better than you, helping someone in need, meditating, or just taking a power nap.

All of the above activities will help in canceling out the stream of negative thoughts that eat you up from inside, and will reset your thinking in a way that makes you move in a much more positive direction.

Meditation and power naps are especially powerful and convenient tools to drastically improve your thinking and, eventually, your circumstances. There is great power in "going dark" and then returning to the hustle-bustle of your daily life.

(Everything in the Universe has emerged from what was once complete darkness. Even today the universe is mostly made up of dark energy and dark matter, and therein lies its power to create galaxies, stars, planets, and, eventually, our circumstances. So, if you want to tap into Universal energy, learn to go *dark*.)

Aim to get at least one power nap or a ten-minute meditation session done every day; it will help you in ways that you cannot even imagine. (Try doing either of them before an important meeting and notice how it unfolds more toward your liking.) Make these two activities a part of your daily routine if you want quick improvements in your life.

Another way to control the mind is by doing an activity so engrossing that it makes you forget about your worries and problems. Find something that you love doing that will make you lose track of time and the world around you. A completely absorbing activity will not only take your attention away from the problems that you are facing, but will also teach you the art of concentration.

When you take your attention away from your problems, they will have no option but to dissipate. The Law of Attraction will not allow things you do not give your attention to, to come into your experience.

Spotting the monkey's patterns

Download a journaling app called MorningPages on your phone, and type 500 words of whatever comes to your mind, first thing in the morning. Take a "brain dump" on this app.

MorningPages will then tell you which thoughts are dominating your brain chatter, and whether they are positive or negative. This will give you a fair idea of whether you are manifesting the good stuff, or the unwanted things, in your life.

After you've tried this app for a while, write down your percentage scores of the first 5 Sundays, here.

Week	Positive or Negative	Percentage
1st Sunday		
2nd Sunday		
3rd Sunday		
4th Sunday		
5th Sunday		

Taming the monkey

Make a list of the engrossing things that can be done by you to bring your focus into the present moment and stop superfluous thoughts.

CHAPTER TEN

UNCLUTTER YOUR SURROUNDINGS

Everything tangible that you see around you is solidified energy—the book you hold in your hands right now, the chair or bed that you may be resting on, the table in your living room, the first person you see in the morning—*absolutely everything is energy*.

And since energy must emit a vibration, everything around you is emitting a vibration. The vibration of a person is much higher than the vibration of an inanimate object, but both of them do emit their own frequencies nonetheless.

When the objects or people around you emit high vibrations, it has a positive effect on your mood. It's why you feel happier around a person who is upbeat, and it's also why you feel better in a house that is clean and well taken care of.

I'm sure you must have heard the phrase "cleanliness is close to godliness" to the point of annoyance, but there is immense truth to that. The big bang (which even many scientists believe was caused by an "unknown power") is one of the many ways to prove that the cleaner and more ordered the things are around you, the higher the vibrations are going to be that surround it. Let me explain.

In physics there is a concept known as entropy, which roughly states that things get more and more chaotic over time. Just before the big bang, the known universe was a tiny condensed ball, which burst out at unfathomable speed to form numerous galaxies, stars, and planets. Even today, the universe is expanding at a much-slower rate, and all the celestial bodies are moving farther away from each other in a haphazard manner. This random, chaotic movement is what is referred to as entropy.

Entropy is not just visible in outer space, but also in your living room, which gets more and more disordered as the day progress (sometimes becoming unrecognizable from what it was in the morning).

What this means is that entropy signifies a gradual reduction in energy. At the time of the big bang, the universe must've needed ridiculous amounts of power to burst out from a tiny ball to almost the size that it is today. Prior to the big bang was when there was absolutely no "clutter" (e.g., stars, planets, asteroids, and black holes) in the universe, and the vibration of the big bang was infinitely greater than the vibration of the universe today.

So, **to increase your vibration and power, bring your house and surroundings as close to their original and uncluttered state as possible.** Throw out all unnecessary items and make serious attempts to make cleanliness and simplicity a priority. The fewer unrequired items you have in your life (including the apps on your cellphone), the faster you will be able to manifest the things you really need.

Clean up and notice the difference in the way you feel. You'll notice immediate improvements in your relationships with your family members when you start uncluttering and freeing up energy. (People are less prone to arguing with each other in an environment that doesn't have too many objects emitting haphazard vibrations of their own.)

The problem with clutter, however, is that it is not always found on the outside. One the biggest obstacles we face on the way to our goals is the clutter within our minds, the clutter that involves past thoughts that have been playing on repeat, unfulfilled wishes, things not worked on, hindering subconscious beliefs, and other ideas that have been thrust upon us. Mental clutter affects 99.99 percent of the people on this planet.

To free yourself from the chaos within your mind, start journaling your thoughts, make a list of things to be worked on in the future, spend time with yourself, and meditate on a daily basis. These activities will go a long way in freeing up your mental space, allowing you to think about the things you really want to experience, and will also help remove most of the thoughts that have been thrust upon you by your interactions with the outside world.

Keep ten to twenty minutes aside, every day, to clean up the clutter in your mind and in your surroundings. This will drastically improve your vibration and, eventually, your ability to manifest the things you desire.

Reducing the clutter

List some of the items in specific areas of your house that haven't been used by you in the past six months.		
Item that hasn't been used in your living room	Do you forsee yourself using it in the next 6 months?	If you did away with it, would it impact your happiness?
Item that hasn't been used in your bedroom	Do you forsee yourself using it in the next 6 months?	If you did away with it, would it impact your happiness?
Item that hasn't been used in your kitchen	Do you forsee yourself using it in the next 6 months?	If you did away with it, would it impact your happiness?

Inviting the good things into your life

List a few adjustments that can be made to your house to make it seem more *inviting*.

CHAPTER ELEVEN

SET UP THE SCENE

Ever notice the amount of mental energy you spend on analyzing and observing the lives of others? So much power within you, and yet you choose to waste it on the people who have so little to do with your life. No wonder your desires don't manifest, and you are forced to read a book like this!

Why not think of yourself as the *lead actor* in this sitcom called *Life*? Why not make this program revolve around you, instead of the millions that surround you? Why waste your production time/budget on peripheral characters? You are the creator of your very own show; shouldn't most of your energies be directed toward shining the spotlight on yourself?

This doesn't mean that you stop caring about your family, friends, and coworkers; all it means is that you **keep the lens focused on your own production and its plot, not the extras in it.**

You can start by looking at everything that you see around you as part of a scene in your personal sitcom. By this measure, most of what you are experiencing today—the set and the actors in front of you—are present in your life because of the scenes you have enacted in the previous seasons of your sitcom, and the direction in which you *chose* to take your story forward.

Some of the seasons may have had different undertones than the rest, but the overall *genre* of the past few years has set the mood for the kind of life you are living today. This genre may or may not have been to your liking, but it most definitely is the reason your life seems to have a *predominant mood* right now.

If you wish to change the mood of your personal TV show, start by making conscious efforts to *set up scenes* in your life that reflect the mood and tone you'd *prefer* to experience. Figure out the genre that is being played out by you today, and decide on the one you'd prefer to play out from now on. Once you've made up your mind about what you'd like to live out in the future seasons of your life, that's when life really starts to get interesting as you move ahead.

The supporting actors, the antagonists, and the leading ladies/men are all going to turn up to audition on their own accord; you do not have much say in who comes in to audition for your sitcom or who wishes to depart. But you *do* have a say in the role that each character plays in your life, how much of the spotlight you wish to shine on each one of them, and the *tone* of your personal TV show.

You could make your life a thriller, drama, comedy, romantic love story, success story, or tragedy; that's completely up to you. If you are in a happy and cheerful mood, your sitcom will gravitate toward being a comedy or a success story; if you are mostly sad and depressed, the sitcom will move toward a tragedy.

Your mood will eventually start affecting the type of actors who come in to audition for parts. A tragedy will attract actors best suited to add to that tone, and a comedy will attract more comedians and people with quick wit. Your frame of mind will also play the biggest part in deciding the top-billed cast of your show.

So, become more conscious and aware of what is being played out in front of you, and act as if you are the director and lead actor of this production. Start visualizing the important scenes in advance, so when you arrive on set, you are familiar with what needs to be done on your part; the supporting cast will have no choice but to adapt to the mood and tone that have been set by you.

When you gain *clarity* about what you want from a particular scene, and your life in general, your personal sitcom will only get better and better. More people will become interested in what you do, production budgets will increase, better actors will come in to audition for parts, your coactors will become more cooperative and less demanding, new seasons will bring with them interesting story lines, and you will feel like the star of this show called *Life*. All it takes is a change of perspective on your part.

What's your genre?

Which of the following would best describe the life that you are experiencing now?	What do you want your life experience to be in the near future?
Adventure	Adventure
Comedy	Comedy
Cooking Show	Cooking Show
Drama	Drama
Fantasy	Fantasy
Office Documentary	Office Documentary
Romance	Romance
Success Story	Success Story
Tragedy	Tragedy
Thriller	Thriller
Violence/Crime	Violence/Crime

Script your life

Lose grip of your current reality and script a scene that you'd like to experience in the near future. Describe all the points in this table in as much detail as possible.

What is the genre of this scene?

What is the backdrop? (Where is it set?)

What is the scene trying to establish in the storyline of your life?

Apart from yourself, which other characters are present?

What can you see, smell, taste, and touch?

What exactly is happening in this scene? (Write a few dialogues if you wish.)

CHAPTER TWELVE

RESPECT THE TEMPLE

Our physical bodies are the vessels through which we accomplish and experience everything here on planet Earth. Without our body's cooperation, performing even the most basic of activities would be a problem, let alone having the energy to enjoy life.

People who make the time to exercise and take pride in their bodies are much better at manifesting the good stuff than the ones who are self-conscious and do not like what they see in the mirror. Our physical health plays the biggest part in affecting the quality of our life.

The quickest and most fail-safe way, then, to increase your vibration is by making exercise a part of your daily routine. Aim to take as many steps as possible in the day, join a gym, go swimming, take the stairs instead of the elevator, park your car slightly far from work, avoid sitting down for extended periods of time, watch your diet, and measure your weight and body fat percentage often; all these activities will help with you becoming the best version of yourself.

Aim to make movement and rest a priority—that's the easiest way of getting fit and eventually speeding up your manifestations. Movement will not only improve your thinking but will also keep the number one enemy—negative thoughts—at bay. Rest, on the other hand, will give you a much-needed break from the mental chatter that plays on repeat, and will direct your thoughts in a more positive direction upon waking.

Whenever you are feeling down and out, either take a power nap or go out for a stroll; you will *always* return in a better mood, and as a changed person, than when you left. Even when you are unsure about whether or not to go ahead with a decision, go for a long walk; it will unfailingly provide you with the answer. Use any excuse to get moving, and notice how quickly you are able to manifest the things you want.

Our bodies are designed to be on the move, not resigned to be seated in front of a screen for the best part of the day. Once you accept this truth and respect your body's need to be in motion, it will always reward you back in terms of a greater sense of self-worth, a better ability to decide on the best possible action to take at every moment, and an increased sense of happiness and well-being.

You'll be amazed with how doors start opening for you when you make conscious efforts to take care of your body. This process will also make you more open to receiving that amazing new relationship that you may be looking for, or in restoring passion in an existing relationship—both of which will skyrocket your vibration and help you manifest even more of the good stuff.

Grooming can also play a big part in inviting in the good stuff. Visit the salon and spa often and pamper yourself; this is your way of thanking your body for how much work it helps you get done here on Earth.

And while you're at it, start dressing yourself in the best possible manner (even when you're at home). Dressing well is the ultimate form of respecting yourself and your body. Receiving a compliment or being noticed by an attractive person can be quite rewarding in terms of how good you feel about yourself. This simple act that lasts a few seconds has the ability to turn your day from negative to positive in an instant, and the kind of clothes you wear and the way you present yourself have a huge impact on the respect you get and attention that comes your way.

Take care of your diet; that, too, plays a major role when it comes to respecting your temple. Food that enters your mouth either increases your vibration or lowers it. Eat as many fruits and vegetables as you can during the day and drink *plenty* of water. Make a mental note of how you feel after you have put something into your mouth; it will give you a fair idea of the effect this food has had on you. (Beware of foods that give you an instant high, such as alcohol, drugs, or black coffee; aim for foods that make you feel good throughout the day.)

Last, but not least, avoid overtiring or taxing yourself; **treat your body like you would treat your best friend**. None of the other manifestations count if you are not in good health; it's what will help you enjoy all the lovely things that enter your life. Revolve your day around making your body feel its best, and watch how your life drastically changes for the better.

Showcasing what you've got

What parts of your body are you most proud of?	What can be done to showcase them? (What kind of clothes/accessories/exercises/adjustments can help?)
1	
2	
3	
4	
5	
6	
7	
8	
9	
10	

Getting there

List the activities that can help you reach your ideal weight. (Even small ones like parking your car slightly far from where you work, or taking the stairs, count.)

CHAPTER THIRTEEN

CHASE NOVELTY

The human mind is designed to love the feelings of novelty and originality; it's a trait that has led our species to discover many new places and conquer the world, prevented us from interbreeding and incest, and led to the invention of various new gadgets, recipes, medicines, and ways of expressing ourselves. It's the *uniqueness of experiencing something new* that makes us feel so good when we do something for the first time.

New parts of the brain light up while doing an activity we've never done before, or when we do the same thing in a different way. The feelings of novelty are the reason why your vibration levels spike on a first date, or when you drive your new car, try something for the first time and end up liking it, or visit a vacation destination you've never been to before. Making conscious efforts to regularly experience something new is a surefire way of keeping your attraction levels at their maximum and maintaining your excitement about life.

When you try something for the first time, your brain gets busy processing this new activity and, for those few seconds, starts developing new neural connections and patterns of thought, making you momentarily abandon any previous thought patterns that may have held you down vibrationally. And it's this feeling of being *in the moment*, to process the impact of this new experience, that makes us feel so good.

Make a note of this: the more novelty that you experience in your life—the more you meet someone new, the more you go to places you've never been to before, the more new clothes you wear, the more ways you come across of expressing yourself professionally, the newer songs/artists you listen to, the more movies you watch or books you read—the better your life will be.

People who live the best lives are those who keep trying something new on a regular basis, and people who live the saddest lives are those who do the same things over and over and over again. **True richness is the ability to experience novelty as often as you can.**

Recognize and embrace this innate need of yours, and do what you can for your brain to experience novelty on a regular basis. Even small things like trying a new route to work, hanging out with different friends, calling for a new dish, learning a new language, reading a new genre of fiction, cultivating a new hobby, discovering parts of your city you've never been to, listening to radio stations you've never heard before, changing your schedule, or doing routine activities in a completely different way will help.

It's important that you get used to the feelings of newness and novelty, because at some point, every manifestation is going to feel new and strange to you. The more open you are to enjoying things for the first time, the more accepting you will become to receiving all that you've been asking for. So, get used to practicing the feelings of novelty as often as you can (while remembering to anchor your day—chapter 7); this will put you on the right energetic track to getting the things you want.

There is a sense of *alertness* that comes with doing something for the *first time*, which few other things can grant you. And it's this alertness that is responsible for bringing you into the present moment and increasing your vibration to heights you may not have experienced before.

Novelty and its benefits

List ten new things that you tried/experienced in the recent past.	
Something new that you consciously experienced:	How alive did it make you feel on a scale of 1–10?
1	
2	
3	
4	
5	
6	
7	
8	
9	
10	

Your novelty index

List the number of times you've done the following in the past year:	Frequency (0, 1–4, 5–10, 10+)
Consciously taken a different route to work	
Made an attempt to talk to someone you didn't know	
Heard the song of an artist you've never listented to before	
Tried out a new cuisine/restaurant	
Taken a new route for your daily walk	
Worn a completely new set of clothes	
Hung out with a new friend	
Cooked something new for yourself	
Tried approaching your work in a completely different way	
Gone to a place you've never been to before	
Read a new book	
Watched a new movie	
Tried a new sport/game	

CHAPTER FOURTEEN

LEARN TO BE SELFISH

Every person on this planet is responsible for creating his or her own reality. The reality that they are experiencing right now may have been chosen by them on a conscious or a subconscious level, but is of their own doing, nonetheless. *You* cannot do anything to undo what people are *choosing* to experience, no matter how hard you try.

If someone feels lonely, it's not your job to make him or her feel good. If someone feels poor, it's not your responsibility to make sure his or her needs are satisfied. If someone is bossing other people, it's not up to you to take matters into your hands and do something about the situation. And if someone isn't doing something the way you think it should be done, it's not productive to bombard that person with advice on what needs to be done.

All you can do is take care of yourself and be an *example* to the people who are going through problems. The best way to have a positive effect on someone's life is by inspiring that person to match up to you.

And to get to that state in which you start inspiring people, you have to learn to be selfish and put your own needs at a priority. No one else is going to go out there and chase your dreams for you; you'll always have to do this yourself. And neither can you chase someone else's dreams for them, or help them in that regard.

So, the next time you are asked to do something by someone that does not serve in your selfish interests, learn to say no without explaining yourself. It's your life; you have all the right to live it exactly the way you'd like.

There is a joy in respecting yourself, putting your self-interests first, prioritizing your needs over the needs of others, and channeling your energies toward bettering your own circumstances, which is unparalleled. This is when all your creative energies are being harnessed in the right direction.

When you try to meddle with someone else's circumstances, or when someone else tries to meddle with yours, there is always going to be a clash or a crossways movement of God / creative energies, which will lead to frustration and the slowing down of manifestations. Why waste your energies mixing them with someone else's, when it only takes your focus away from what's really important in life?

Everything else (and I mean *absolutely* everything else) will fall into place beautifully, once you start pleasing yourself and putting your needs first. Remember that at any point, you are either doing something to please yourself, or you are doing something to please someone else; there are no in-betweens in this game.

You cannot do something to please someone else and be happy at the same time, or even expect your desires to come to you, for that matter. That would defy the powerful Law of Attraction.

Learn to **help a person or do something for others only if it makes you feel good, not because there is an obligation for you to do so**. Most people will almost always find a way, with or without your support, and you will be glad you spent your time doing things that really matter.

People pleasing and its pitfalls

List three things you did just to please *someone else:*	How did you feel at the end of it, on a scale of 1–10?	Did it lead to something better?
List three things you did to please *yourself*:	How did you feel at the end of it, on a scale of 1–10?	Did it lead to something better?

You deserve the good stuff

List ten reasons you are better, and more worthy of getting the things you want, than most people you know.

1

2

3

4

5

6

7

8

9

10

CHAPTER FIFTEEN

CAST YOUR SPELLS

There is so much power in the words that come out of a person's mouth, that literally anything said out loud is like a spell that gets cast on his or her life. The subconscious always responds to the things we talk about, and is alert 24/7, so consistently speaking words of abundance and positivity is the *only* way we can get the subconscious to start moving our life in that direction.

So many are unaware of the things they say until it really starts affecting their lives. Complaining and joking about how bad life is has really become the norm these days, which further gives birth to circumstances that lead to more opportunities to complain and joke about.

One of the best ways of reversing the damage that has been done by years of complaining/conditioning, and removing the blocks that have been preventing us from attaining our desires, is by drilling the *opposite of what has been holding us down* into our conscious mind, on a regular basis, through the use of affirmations.

I'm sure you've heard about affirmations before and may be tired of how many LOA teachers propagate their use (I am), but affirmations are immensely popular today because of how useful they are. Think of them as the toothpaste of the Law of Attraction world; they are that important, commonplace, useful, and easy to apply.

What the repetition of a few words said out loud (in a way that makes your desires seem within reach) does is that it imprints your desire onto your subconscious mind. The deeper and more powerful part of your brain then starts working its magic, and results soon start becoming apparent (especially if you affirm your desires just before you sleep and the first thing upon waking).

Affirmations are so powerful when repeated regularly that even if you repeatedly affirm "I am a chimpanzee," you'll notice that your behavior becomes more apelike and irrational (not that I've tried it, but I'm sure it does the trick).

The good news is that you can affirm absolutely anything you want and expect results. Try affirming that "I am a God/Goddess" for a few weeks, every day for a few minutes, and notice the difference in how you feel.

The best thing about affirmations is that they are malleable and versatile and can be used for absolutely anything. If you want to improve your relationship with someone, you can affirm, "My relationship with this person is improving every day," and expect to see the results. If you want to become better at a sport, you can affirm, "Every day and in every way I am getting better and better at this sport," and your teammates will also start noticing the difference. If you want a raise at work (who doesn't!), you can affirm, "The raise I deserve is rightly coming to me, as my boss notices the value I add to his/her organization."

Absolutely anything that you say repeatedly becomes an affirmation of sorts. If you are constantly complaining about your boss, you are in a way *affirming* that you have a bad boss, and your subconscious will have to go out of its way to make sure that your boss *continues* to behave the way he does around you. But if you speak about how lucky you are in life, the subconscious will line up circumstances to reflect that.

Watching your words can be very hard to begin with—just like watching your diet. It's as if you've been eating (saying) junk all this while, and suddenly a dietician is telling you to stop eating (saying) these things. So, instead of attempting to only speak words of positivity, try using affirmations for five minutes every day. Use affirmations like you would take a multivitamin, then slowly start making conscious efforts to watch what you say during other periods of the day.

The Universe has given you the power to create absolutely anything you want through your thoughts, words, and actions. Thoughts are the abstract bit that are hard to measure and track; actions are very concrete and require effort on your part, but it's your words that create a bridge between your thoughts and actions and connect all three. Words are the magical part of the trinity that truly set things into motion.

Pay attention to the words that come out of your mouth, and your thoughts, and actions will automatically improve. When you have the three elements of creation working positively, miracles will become commonplace, and you'll begin to feel the effortlessness and joy of life.

Tailoring your affirmations

Which part of your life would you like to improve the most? (Circle the most appropriate one)					
Health	Wealth	Relationships	Community Service	Professional	Success, Spiritual Progress

Now, write down the exact thing you want to improve in this area. (If it's wealth, write down how much you'd like your bank account balance to be at the end of the year. If it's Professional Success, write down the position you'd like to be in at the end of the year.)

Create an affirmation for the above as if you've already received it, giving thanks to the Universe.

[I, (your name), thankfully accept the (exact) money that has flown effortlessly into my bank account]

Pay attention to the way you are feeling. If reciting the above makes you feel good, say it for 5 minutes every night before you sleep.

If saying it brings out a feeling of lack in you, or makes you feel as if your desire hasn't arrived yet, then just recite the key word (amount of money if it's Wealth that you want to improve) without saying anything else, i.e., $50,000, $50,000, $50,000 $50,000, and visualize the $50,000 being credited to your bank account as you affirm.

The power of compliments

List five people who have helped you the most in the recent past, and the last time you complimented them on something.

Person	Last time you complimented them	What else could you compliment them on?
1		
2		
3		
4		
5		

You will be surprised with how powerful a compliment can be in improving your relationship with absolutely anyone.

CHAPTER SIXTEEN

USE THE POWER OF MUSIC

There is something otherworldly about the nature of music that has this amazing ability to make us forget about our worries or life circumstances that may be less than ideal and help us project a much better future than what we've been currently imagining. I haven't come across a single person who hasn't benefited massively from music in some way.

Not only is music one of the most powerful manifestational tools, it is also a medium through which our deepest thoughts find expression in a beautiful way. And on a subliminal level, it makes us realize that not all is wrong with the world, and that there are people out there who want to make our lives beautiful through their songs and self-expression.

Apart from being inexpensive for most, music also gives us a sense of community and kills our loneliness. Make it an integral part of your life, and you will see very quick results in your manifestation game. Buy a new pair of headphones, get a music subscription, download and listen to songs and artists from various genres, share songs you like with your friends and encourage them to do the same, listen to radio stations from across the world, pick up and learn an instrument, and sing with the people you like hanging out with; you'll be amazed with how this spikes your vibration and puts you in a wonderful place that allows the manifestations in.

Good songs have the ability to not just bring your attention to the present moment, but also to put you in a state of ecstasy—a state in which you don't care whether the manifestations you are seeking come about or not. And paradoxically, that's when the magic happens.

The quality of your life will increase exponentially with every new song/artist you discover and enjoy. Make a list of the artists you love listening to, and aim to expand it by at least three new entrées every year. Finding music you fall in love with is like discovering manifestational gold mines; it is bound to give you the vibrational currency you seek.

Discover and explore new music as often as you can. You may not connect with everything you hear, but when you *do* come across something you really like, the next few days are going to be really good for you. This new song will now form the base of your vibration for the days that lie ahead, lurking behind your conscious mind and reminding you that everything is actually all right. Play such tracks on repeat; they will help smooth out even the roughest parts of your life.

Make the avenues of your music your best friend and use them as often as you can to raise your vibration. Plan special trips/walks/getaways just to hear new music that comes out; it'll be one of the most satisfying things you will ever experience. And look at all new music or musical equipment that you purchase as an investment, not an expense; its rewards in terms of serotonin (a.k.a. manifestational juice) released will far outweigh the costs.

There really are only two kinds of days in life—the days you enjoy music . . . and the days you don't. The former is when it seems like you are floating and oblivious to your worries, and the latter is when you are not using your manifestational powers to their maximum.

When you lose yourself to the music you really like, you catch glimpses of the vibratory states of higher dimensions—states in which manifesting the things you want is a piece of cake. Take every opportunity you can to generate such feelings within you; few other things will be able to give you the same amount of bliss.

Your goldmines

List ten artists you love listening to:
1
2
3
4
5
6
7
8
9
10

The all-time favorites

Make a list of ten songs that have given you the most amount of happiness over the years:

Song	Artist	Album
1		
2		
3		
4		
5		
6		
7		
8		
9		
10		

Make a playlist of this on your media player and listen to it at least once a month.

CHAPTER SEVENTEEN

CUT YOUR COMMUTE

Probably one of the biggest drains on our energy is the traffic that so many of us have to endure on a daily basis just to get to work. Traffic, or chaos in general, always incites strong negative emotion within the person stuck in it, and this unfailingly reduces his or her vibration. These feelings of being "stuck" then spill over to other parts of our lives, affecting our relationships as well.

So, if you really want to live a balanced, healthy, productive, and peaceful life, you need to find ways to cut down on the time you spend on your commute. Not only will this free up mental space to think about the good things that your professional life has to offer, but it will also prevent you from getting stressed even before your workday has begun.

A positive and tranquil start to your day will make it more likely for you to put your best foot forward at work, improve your relationship with your colleagues, increase the chances of you rising up in your organization, prevent you from facing an early burnout in your career, and make you enjoy your life more.

A relaxed start would also result in the Law of Attraction being tipped in your favor at the very beginning of your day, and this would generally lead to your entire morning segment being positive and upbeat, providing you with a solid foundation for the entire day.

A smaller commute time would also result in less anxiety toward the end of your workday—the time when you just want to wind up your work and go home to relax. Knowledge of the fact that your home isn't that far away (in terms of the time it takes to reach) and that you can do as you please once you get there, will help you power through the last bit of what is expected of you in the day, even when your energies may be sapped due to mental fatigue. A short commute will also provide you with the incentive to finish your tasks faster, prevent you from taking your work home, and improve your social life.

Not only are the people who face a smaller commute happier with their life in general, but they also get the time to hit the gym or go for long walks once they're back home, they are more available for their family and friends, and they tend to remain longer at their companies or organizations during their careers. Make the travel time a priority when thinking about your next job, and your happiness levels will increase drastically.

There are a number of ways in which you can free yourself from the chaos of the commute: You can leave early for work, leave early from work, take local transportation instead of your car, work from home, request a different shift, find work close to your home, or find a living arrangement close to your place of work. These adjustments will go a long way in making your life feel abundant and balanced.

I would even suggest that you walk or cycle to work, if it is feasible for you to do so. Ten thousand steps are what most experts recommend we walk on a daily basis to meet our fitness quotas; most of us get nothing close to that figure thanks to our sedentary lifestyles. Walking to work (or part of the way) is a surefire way of meeting your daily steps requirement.

Getting a good walk even before you start your workday is also one of the best feelings, and these feelings of productivity/pride are bound to reflect in the quality and quantity of your work. Besides saving a fortune on gas, you will also save on medical expenses in the future. Give this a shot when the weather in your city supports walking the most, and notice your manifestations at the end of the month; you'll be surprised with the avalanche of good things that come your way.

Ultimately, freedom is the basis for living a happy life. The less time you spend in traffic, the freer you will feel, and ideas on how to improve your life's circumstances will come to you very quickly.

Freeing up your time

How many hours in the day do you spend travelling?		
(0 –1)	(1–3)	(3–5)
List the things you can do to bring this figure down.		

Get moving

How many miles do you walk in the week?			
(0–1)	(1–5)	(5–10)	(10+)

List the things that can be done to bring this number up. (Walking to work, walking at work, walking in the park, taking the stairs instead of the elevator, parking your car slightly away from your place of work, joining a gym.)

CHAPTER EIGHTEEN

TUNE YOUR FREQUENCIES

Want to hear something mind-blowingly amazing?

Everything that you desire today, or could desire in the future, already exists as a reality and is being experienced by a greater part of you right now.

The reason you don't actually see this happening is because your desires are vibrating at frequencies very different from what you are vibrating at in this current moment. It's your tuning in relation to your desire that either grants you access to it or keeps it hidden from you.

The higher you vibrate, the more accessible all the things you want will be to you, and the lower your frequencies, the more they will begin to feel like a distant dream.

When you reach the really high frequencies, you won't even have to put in efforts to get your desires; *they* will make their way to you (that's how cool this whole manifestation game is). But you *have to* do your bit and tune yourself to those frequencies to see this whole "desires making their way to you" thing firsthand.

And the easiest way to start vibrating at the level of your desires is by arranging your life in such a way that your happiness does not *depend* on your desires coming to fruition. The manifestations you are after should feel like the *icing* on the cake of your life, not the cake itself. That's the optimum and most powerful stance with which you can create the life you want.

Most people are unaware of this truth because they do not pay attention to the way their strongest desires magically unfold for them, seemingly out of nowhere, when they are happy and enjoying life. Being on the happy frequencies is what takes us closer to the reality we'd prefer to be living.

But since frequency and vibration are things we human beings cannot measure, we have to look at what's coming our way to know which frequency we are on. To get a grip on what I'm talking about, think of your life as a radio transmitter, your current circumstances as the radio station you are tuned to and the manifestations as the songs that come out of it.

What you are experiencing right now in your life is simply a result of the radio station you are currently tuned to. If you are unhappy with your life at the moment, it's because you have your dial set on frequencies that do not match the frequencies of the kind of life you desire. And if your life seems amazing, it definitely means that you are on the right track to getting *even more* of the things you want.

Everything that you are experiencing in your life right now is because you are on the same frequency / radio station as what's coming your way. This station may dish out a few manifestations that you like, but if it's not your preferred station, chances are that you are not going to like most of the other manifestations that it produces.

The happier you become with your life, the closer you will get to the radio station / lifestyle you desire, and the better your manifestations will become. At first, you will begin to notice small improvements in your life, giving you a clear indication that you are moving toward the life you want. And as you start making a conscious note of these improvements, it will give you even more motivation to continue your vibrational work and move up the frequency scale.

Instead of trying to force your desires to come to you quickly, always focus on increasing your frequencies; it will take you to the things you want, much faster. All the small things you made a list of in chapter 1 will help with this.

Start seeing everything you want as energy vibrating at different frequencies. The boyfriend/girlfriend, dream house, beach vacation, relaxed and lucrative job, ideal family life, vacation home, second vacation home, fame, success—everything is there for you to experience, but vibrating at frequencies that are currently inaccessible to you. All you have to do to be able to *tangibly* experience these things in your life is learn to become happy with or without them.

The effect of frequencies

Make a list of the 10 best things that happened to you in the recent past, and your state of mind at the time.

Manifestation that occurred	Activity you were doing when this manifestation occurred	How good were you feeling on a scale of 1–10?
1		
2		
3		
4		
5		
6		
7		
8		
9		
10		

Getting there

Aspect of your life	What would you like to manifest at the end of the year? (Assign this manifestation a score of 100)	Where are you right now in terms of this manifestation? (Assign a score on a scale of 1–100 based on how good you are *feeling* about it—not on what has/has not happened in real life)
For the most important area of your life (wealth, relationships, or health), write down what you would like to manifest at the end of the year.		
		Now -
		Month 1 -
		Month 2 -
		Month 3 -
		Month 4 -
		Month 5 -
		Month 6 -
		Month 7 -
		Month 8 -
		Month 9 -
		Month 10 -
		Month 11 -

CHAPTER NINETEEN

MIND YOUR OWN BUSINESS

If you hold a sincere desire within your heart, the Universe has the means to deliver this desire to you, *regardless* of the family you were born into, the people you are connected to, the information you may or may not possess about this desire, or the circumstances that surround you in this current moment. There is nothing outside you that can reduce, or even increase, your ability to get the things you want. All the power we possess is within us.

The only reason, then, why *some* go on to live the life of their dreams, while others make do with what-is, is because the former direct most of their attention toward the improvement of their own life, while the latter waste energy obsessing about and observing the people or circumstances that surround them.

And to get to the level of those select few master manifesters, you too have to learn to be selective about what you give your attention to, and practice the art of minding your own business. This way, you learn to direct your precious mental energy on the things *you would* prefer to experience, and not on what goes on around you.

Where thought goes, energy flows; so, before you think about some person or event, ask yourself if it deserves your attention, which could otherwise have been used to better your own life. Very rarely will improving your personal circumstances require giving thought to something outside your control.

Being able to *harness* the powerful mental energy available to you at all times, in a way that directs it inward and for the betterment of one's life, is the key to getting your circumstances to improve more rapidly than they ever have before.

We all are so used to having our energies scattered that it takes awhile for us to start redirecting them from what goes on around us toward the things we desire. And with the improvements in technology and the advent of social media, our attention spans have reduced even further, scattering our energies like never before.

Distractions are why many of us are finding it harder, today, to manifest the things we want, and we are feeling as if we are missing out on life. By giving our attention to things outside us, rather than on the things we desire, we slow down the speed with which we are able to manifest these things.

Aim to cut down even on the amount of time you spend watching television or browsing social media sites, and notice how your desires start gaining momentum. Use distractions like these only when you find yourself thinking too many negative thoughts about a particular event. Distractions can be advantageous when you are stressed, worried, confused, or feeling hopeless; the rest of the time they just divert your powerful creative energies.

When you feel the need to be entertained, pick up a notebook and start writing the things you really like about your life—and *why you like them*. This will teach you to focus on the things that are really working for you in your life and, by the powerful Law of Attraction, to bring more of them into your experience. Writing about the things you love is one of the best ways to keep yourself occupied and create the life you desire at the same time.

As you learn to direct your energies toward your own circumstances and the things that make you *feel good*, the time you feel stressed/worried/confused/hopeless will start reducing, and your desire for entertainment will also reduce once this shift occurs. When you realize how powerful your attention and ability to create are, your main source of entertainment will be looking forward to your next manifestation, and then the next, and then the next; your life will then become your main source of entertainment!

If you only knew how powerful and deserving you were, giving the kind of importance you do to the things that do not concern you wouldn't seem as appealing as it does to you now.

Once you become aware of what you are capable of achieving, you will start considering *yourself* to be the rock star of your life and **make things revolve around the way you feel—not what others say, think, feel, or go through.**

Too much information?

Source of entertainment/ information	When was the last time you gained something valuable from this source? (Today/Last Week/Two Weeks Ago/Last Month/Six Months Ago)	How did you use this information to improve your life?
Gossip/Hearsay		
News Channel		
Newspaper		
Social Media		
Magazines		
Sports Broadcasts		

Giving up on the gossip

List five people you hang out with the most, and their propensity to talk about others.	
Friend/Family Member	Propensity to gossip on a scale of 1–10
1	
2	
3	
4	
5	

If the total score on the right is above 25, you'd be better off making new friends, for your own sake

CHAPTER TWENTY

PRACTICE EQUANIMITY

All right, by now you've read a fair share of this book and gotten a grasp of how the Law of Attraction works, hopefully manifesting many lovely things in the process. But that's only part of the game.

The first step toward living a happy life is being clear about what you want. The second step is actually manifesting that desire. The third crucial step is *maintaining the vibration with which you attracted this desire* and not getting overwhelmed once it manifests in your life.

Getting overwhelmed / overexcited / extra happy about the fact that your desire has come to you *dampens* the high vibration with which you attracted the desire in the first place. This is your way of telling your subconscious, "This manifestation is too much for me to handle. Bring me down to the vibration level I am used to." And your subconscious has no option but to get to work and create problems with this manifestation or retard its advance toward you.

If something feels like a "big deal," it means you are holding yourself apart from the desire, and even if you *do* manage to manifest it into your life, chances are it's not going to remain for very long. Your subconscious won't appreciate this "big" new thing in your life because it isn't used to those kinds of frequencies and will look to pull you down to familiar territory.

Which is why there is great power in maintaining equanimity, even when all your desires are being fulfilled. Equanimity is your way of communicating to the Universe that this new manifestation isn't a big deal at all, and in a way also telling it, "Show me what else you got!" That is when the Universe begins to yield much more of the good stuff to you.

When you consider the size of the Universe and how expansive it is compared to the desires you hold in your heart, you'll realize that all the things you've been asking for are nothing compared to what the Universe is capable of producing and delivering.

If multiple galaxies can be created out of nothing but darkness in a short burst of time, do you think a couple of brand-new cars would be a problem for the Universe? Yet, most of us have a tendency to get overexcited when the first car comes our way, thereby reducing the speed with which the second is manifested.

The reason a second car is harder for most to manifest than, say, a cup of coffee is because we attach such a high value to the car that its manifestation seems impossible or a really big deal. The cup of coffee, on the other hand, doesn't seem that big a deal at all; you continue to maintain your composure even after you receive it (unless, of course, you consume copious amounts of coffee in one sitting). Learn to **take the "cup-of-coffee" approach" to everything you want to manifest in your life; nothing should seem like a big deal.**

Meditation can really help reaching such a state in which things outside you seem trivial. It is one of the rare activities that can make you reach a state of *detachment*, where you learn to look at everything that you've manifested, from a distance, making you less prone to becoming worried about losing the things you have or extra proud about the fact that you've manifested them. Meditation is what will take you to the "Show me what else you got!" state.

So, for the sake of your desires and their continuous flow toward you, learn to maintain your composure and keep your wits about you even when things are going exceedingly well, and your life seems like a dream; this is a vibrational habit that will serve you very well in the manifestation game. Enjoy your desires *slowly* and let them unfold for you on their own accord; relish the unfolding of your desire as much as its eventual manifestation. And always aim to take action *from* a state of peace, not *to* reach a state of peace.

When you realize how worthy you are just because you exist, you'll understand why there is no need for you to become overly happy when you manifest something good in your life. Your desires are meant to come to you (you wouldn't have them in your heart if they didn't have your name written on them); there really is no other way. And the more relaxed you are about your desires, the faster they will come; the more overexcited you get, the wobblier the whole process is going to seem.

Too good to be true?

When was the last time a desire felt "really big" for you, or "too good to be true"? And what was it?

How long did it last? Did it last longer or shorter than you expected it to?

Did you take any "extra" (i.e. unrequired) action to prevent it from going away? And did it help?

Too good AND true

Write down your #1 desire:
Now write down all the reasons you deserve this desire, more than anyone else.
Look at this list often.

CHAPTER TWENTY-ONE

DEFY GRAVITY

Want to hear something reassuring?

Those negative thoughts that go on in your head—the ones that eat you up from inside—aren't your fault at all. They are just a side effect of the way we are designed as a species.

We are all descendants of human beings who survived the dangers of the wild because they were paranoid and afraid of the dangers lurking around them. Those paranoid thoughts were what kept them on guard and safe from predators.

Imagine if our prehistoric ancestors had just *chilled* and thought peaceful thoughts; what do you think would have happened to our kind? We'd be wiped out by the fiercer animals, right? It's the fearful and negative thoughts that made us survive and the positive thoughts that made our numbers grow.

What I am trying to convey is that it is absolutely normal for you to think bad thoughts! In fact, it just means you are more alert than the others and instinctively want to protect yourself. These thoughts only occur to you because you are genetically structured to think that way.

So, the next time you catch yourself thinking a stream of bad thoughts, don't beat up on yourself. Just realize that your brain will *always* gravitate toward them as a self-serving mechanism, in a bid to protect itself from harm.

Only a *few* are able to consistently deny this tendency of unnecessarily thinking bad thoughts and to move toward the life of their dreams. It's almost as if these people have mastered gravity, thanks to their mental discipline, and can now fly to wherever they want. For the rest, life just seems to go from bad to worse because the gravity of their thoughts keeps pulling them down; it's only natural.

All you need to do, then, to drastically improve the quality of your life, is inculcate the mental discipline of avoiding the negative mental chatter—as much as possible. You do not even need to think good thoughts or thoughts of abundance; **all you need to do is avoid thinking bad thoughts; positivity will automatically make its way to you.**

Pay attention to the negative thoughts that go on in your mind, and stop it before it gains momentum. Just like you would deflect unpleasant conversations that would come up on the dinner table, deflect such unpleasant conversations in your head as well.

You may not find this discipline easy to begin with (just like a rocket finds it hardest to escape the Earth's gravity at the beginning of its launch), but once you get the hang of it, life will seem like a dream, and you'll be cruising toward your desires at massive speeds.

Distraction, meditation, and having a job that you really enjoy are excellent ways of defying the tendency to think bad thoughts. When you find yourself thinking too many negative thoughts, meditate, go to a movie, meet with positive friends, get outdoors, try something new, strike a conversation with a stranger, or search for a job that you would love to do; all of these will help change the direction of your thoughts for the better.

Remember that at any time, you are either thinking a thought that produces a positive emotion or a thought that produces a negative one; there is no such thing as a neutral thought that doesn't produce any emotion at all. Some thoughts produce weaker emotional states (boredom, pessimism, lethargy, hope) than others (passion, love, hatred, rage), but some emotion is *always* produced. And if you aren't thinking a thought that produces a negative emotion, then, by default, there is positive emotion being produced within you!

If you can just stop yourself from being pulled down by your own mind, it's going to feel like you're floating.

Getting into a meditative state

List five times you went into a meditative state (were in the zone) in the past, and what you were doing at the time.

Time you went into a meditative state	Corresponding activity
1	
2	
3	
4	
5	

This is the state in which you float.

Avoiding the high gravity zones

Download an app called MorningPages on your smartphone, and type 500 words of whatever comes to your mind, first thing upon waking. The app will then give you a score, letting you know how happy or sad you are in the moment.

On the mornings you get a negative score, make a note of what you did the previous day to get such a score, and avoid doing that again.

Day on which you got a negative score	What do you think led to this score? (Be brief)	What else can you do instead?

CHAPTER TWENTY-TWO

VENT YOUR ANGER

Anger is one of the most powerful human emotions, which, if suppressed, could lead to serious mental and physical issues that have long-term effects on our health. It unfailingly finds a way to express itself, regardless of how much you try to control or suppress the emotion—anger *always* needs an outlet.

The most miserable people today are the ones who've been taught that it's wrong for them to express this basic emotion and sacrifice it in order to get along with the people around them. The problem with this is that their anger then gets directed inward and manifests itself in the form of depression and other self-destructive tendencies.

Of course there are going to be repercussions when you express your anger, but the repercussions of bottling it up are far worse. Not being able to express this basic emotion is like swallowing poison—it only harms you and the ones you love. The key is to express it as soon as possible without allowing it to grow and multiply within you, which may cause an unnecessarily large reaction later.

At times you are going to be faced with a difficult choice of either expressing your anger and facing the repercussions that may arise (which may hurt temporarily) or holding on to it and letting it slowly poison you. Whenever possible, be brave enough to choose the former.

Ever noticed kids and how expressive they are? When they love someone, they show it, and when they are angry with someone—they express it! It's why they are so happy and free of any form of depression; they never bottle up any of their emotions. This is a quality that makes them so joyful and full of energy. And it's also what allows them to sleep peacefully at night, because they just don't hold on to things like we do.

But as we grow up, we are taught that it is *wrong* for us to express what we are going through, and that's when the bottling up and poisoning begins. We are taught to suppress our emotions in favor of what society expects of us, and in the process we sacrifice our authenticity so others can feel happy and secure.

Bottling up your emotions is one of the biggest vibrational dampeners; it just pulls you down. Express your anger when it gives you a sense of relief (e.g., when it pulls you out of a depressed state); universal energies will always support you when this is the case. *Do not* express your anger out of *habit* or to show your *authority* to someone.

Human emotions are perfect as they are. Stay true to yourself and express your anger when you feel you have been wronged; you will save yourself a lot of future turmoil. And never feel guilty about anything that you do, no matter what society forces you to think. Society has no clue about what caused you to react in a particular way or about the circumstances that led up to the event. **Learn to respect yourself and the emotions bubbling inside you; it's the only way you'll find peace.**

Sometimes a person may have wronged you in the past, and nothing much can be done now to express your anger against this person. This is where journaling, talking to a therapist, or venting out your anger in the gym or a kickboxing class can really help you. Make serious attempts to find ways of channeling your anger when you feel it isn't getting an outlet.

A good way to avoid future incidents that may anger you, altogether, is by prepaving a particular section of your day before you actually live it. Visualize that part of your day going smoothly and efficiently, beforehand.

If you know that going to work may result in feelings of anger, or interacting with a particular coworker might test your patience, visualize yourself keeping the interaction with this coworker quick and minimal. This way you won't entertain any unnecessary nonsense and would have prepaved your interactions with him or her. You can do this for almost any part of your day; it will improve the overall quality of your life like never before.

Venting out

List ten ways you can get anger out of your system. (Journalling your thoughts, on a punching bag, joining a kickboxing class, lifting weights in the gym, running on a treadmill, speaking with a therapist)	
Activity that can help you vent your anger:	How many times have you done it in the recent past? (0–5, 5–10, 10+)
1	
2	
3	
4	
5	
6	
7	
8	
9	
10	

List ten things you can do to feel *powerful*.
(Helping those in need, public speaking, running, wearing clothes that make you feel authoritative, walking like you own the place, asserting yourself in subtle yet noticeable ways, requesting for a premium parking spot, making new friends, lifting weights in the gym, volunteering for a political party, etc.)

1

2

3

4

5

6

7

8

9

10

CHAPTER TWENTY-THREE

SCULPTED GRATITUDE

No Law of Attraction book would be complete without a chapter on one of the most powerful and popular techniques of them all—gratitude.

Appreciating what is good about your life is what brings even more of these wonderful things into your experience. This is, and will always be, the crux of every LOA book you will ever read.

It's simple, really; when you take notice of the aspects of your experience that are to your liking, you attract even more of them by the power of your attention, focus, and energy. And when you *make it a habit* to look for what you really like, appreciate, and are thankful for, your life's circumstances just keep getting better and better until you *only* have things you are thankful for. Serial appreciation of what is good about your life is the best way to get it to improve like never before.

One especially powerful technique that can help speed up your manifestations by using the power of appreciation, or improve a *specific* area of your life that may not be to your liking, is what I call Sculpted Gratitude. This is a process by which you *purposely create* a particular aspect of your experience, by thanking the Universe *in the direction* in which you want this area of your life to move toward.

Here's how it works. Let's assume you are feeling lonely and miserable and really want someone to share your life with. Now, in order to get your life moving that way, start sculpting your thank-you notes in the opposite direction of what you are currently experiencing. At the end of the day or week, reflect back on all the *small* instances in which you felt loved, and write thank-you notes for it.

This means even if someone made genuine eye contact with you, make a note of this in your Sculpted Gratitude journal. Or if an attractive person held the door for you while you walked behind them, you could mention this too. Or maybe someone you had a crush on in high school liked your comment on social media; make a note of this and say thank you to the Universe!

By intentionally focusing on the opposite of what you hate about your life, you give the Universe no choice but to slowly start changing your life's circumstances to reflect this change of perspective. Once you start applying this process and make conscious efforts to give thanks for what you most want to improve, you will soon begin to notice visible changes in your life.

The beauty of the Sculpted Gratitude technique is that it can be used for absolutely any area of your life. If you are feeling powerless and weak, sculpt your thank-you notes in the direction of power. Thank the universe for every small instance during the day in which you felt powerful and someone gave you respect. Then, watch how your power and influence slowly begin to grow.

If you are feeling poor and lacking in abundance, start by thanking the Universe for all the instances in which you felt rich. Make a mental note of every single dollar that came your way that day or week and give thanks for it. Even if this means that you got a discount on your grocery bill, consider that as income and give thanks for it. If your spouse or parent paid a common bill, consider that as income in your gratitude journal. Every small thing that made you feel rich could go into this journal of yours.

If you are feeling stuck and lacking in the amount of freedom that you would like to experience, make a note of all the instances in which you could do absolutely what you wanted to during the day. Even if it means listening to songs of your choosing on your way back home after a long day at work, make a note of it. The privilege of having a desk of your own and getting to arrange your stationery the way you want to is also worthy of mentioning.

Giving attention to something means diverting life energy toward it. And by purposely energizing those aspects of your life that you'd prefer to experience, you increase the frequency/regularity with which you experience them.

Once you start witnessing improvements in the areas you are consciously giving energy to, you will want to write more and more thank-you notes in that direction to keep the momentum going. Eventually, you will reach a point where you no longer feel lack in that aspect of your life.

Love sculpting

Write down ten small instances in which you felt loved, in the past week.
1
2
3
4
5
6
7
8
9
10

Getting what you want

What would you like to experience the most of, in the near future? (Circle it)
Excitement
Friendships
Health
Power
Recognition
Romance
Wealth
Freedom
Maintain a sculpted gratitude journal for the above, and write in it as often as you can. Take notice of the smallest of activities that reflect what you would like to experience, and thank the Universe for it. Even if you have to exaggerate some of the thank-you notes, it will work towards bringing you more of what you want.

CHAPTER TWENTY-FOUR

GET USED TO SAYING NO

One of the biggest vibrational dampeners is the feeling of being *obligated* to do the things you really don't want to do, in a way that your freedom gets compromised.

The ability to pursue the activities you love, *when* you feel like pursuing them, is not just the true measure of abundance, but also the key to living a happy life. And this freedom to do the things you love doing is something that you have to claim for yourself; it isn't something that gets handed to you.

Doing what you *really* want to do multiplies your energy, and acting under obligation drains you out. People who feel low and tired most of the time are the ones who spend a good part of their day fulfilling the requests that have been thrust on them, and using their energies in trying to please others.

People-pleasing is an affliction that affects so many of us because of our tendency to act out of fear instead of love. Most of us wrongly think that saying NO to a person might affect our future circumstances in a negative way, when, really, only our vibrational levels, and the way we feel in a given moment, are what create our circumstances.

Putting others' needs ahead of our own, by always saying yes to the demands that are being thrust on us, causes our energy levels to dip like nothing else and must be avoided at all costs.

Learn to put yourself first and say NO to people's selfish requests on your time or energy when it does not serve you in some way. Not only will you do yourself a favor, but you will also do the person making the request a massive favor by not inflicting your conflicted energies to the task at hand. It will also drastically increase your ability to manifest the things you want, since you no longer divert your energies on tasks that you want nothing to do with.

Practice saying "no thanks" in front of the mirror without feeling the need to explain yourself. There is immense power in those two words, and they have the ability to give you the *freedom* to create the life you want. The first few times you say them, you are bound to feel guilty about it, but once you get the hang of it, you will sense the freedom that accompanies these purposeful words, and the role they can play in improving your life.

Extend this practice of saying NO even to the *conversations* that you do not wish to have. If someone brings up a serious topic that you may not be in the mood to discuss, or a topic that makes you uncomfortable, refuse to engage in such a discussion.

This is one of the best ways of protecting your energies and making sure you don't get dragged down by someone else.

Usually, we are very good at saying NO to people we love the most, but succumb to the request of someone we don't really know that well—when it really should be the other way around. Outsiders always keep their personal interests in mind first.

Every grown and healthy person has the capacity to help himself and take on any challenge that comes his way; you do not need to compromise your time to be of service to anyone else. Tend to your vibrational levels first, and everything around you will reflect your improved state of being. (When you are vibrating at high levels, you won't even get unnecessary requests asking you to do things you really don't want to.)

You will instantly feel your energy lift when you give a clear-cut NO as an answer to something you don't feel like doing; it is one of the best power statements and lets the other person know that you are aware of your worth.

You are the creator of your own reality; you get to decide how you want to live your life. If something is making you feel restricted in some way, you have played your part in manifesting it by trying to please others. NO is the magic word that will start filling your life with the freedom that you crave and deserve, and move you much closer to the things you really desire.

Are you standing up for yourself?

How comfortable do you feel doing the following? On a scale of 1–10, how comfortable are you with the following?	
Saying NO to people	
Delegating a task to someone who has more time to handle it	
Letting someone know that you are not happy when they force something on you	
Cancelling plans if you don't feel like going ahead with them	
Standing up for yourself when you feel the need to	
A total score of less than 25 means that you really need to start putting your own needs ahead of others'	

The pointlessness of putting others first

List five things you did just because you couldn't say NO:		
Something you did just because you couldn't say NO	Could someone else have done it?	Did your presence really make a noticeable difference to the outcome?
1		
2		
3		
4		
5		

CHAPTER TWENTY-FIVE

GET YOURSELF ON THE RIGHT ADDRESS

Every time you have a clear desire about wanting to experience something, the first step toward getting what you want is *already done*. Think of the whole process as placing an order on Universe.com; you identify what you want from the Universe's catalog and make a request for it to be delivered to you. The Universe, then, immediately starts leveraging all its resources to package and present this order of yours to your doorstep.

After that, all you have to do is *get yourself on the right energetic address* to receive this desire, because the Universe does not understand physical addresses; it only understands energy. Once you get yourself on the right energetic address (that is, you've reached a state where you don't *need* this desire to be happy), you will find your package waiting for you to enjoy it.

And you'll know you've reached the right address when the unavailability of your desire does not bother you any more or play on your conscious mind most of the time; but rather, the majority of your thoughts are about the things that are going really well in your life. This is a state in which your vibrational levels are higher than that of your desire, and therefore it is within your reach.

So, the next time you really want something, set out an intention to the Universe (place your order by writing it down in a notebook or visualizing it) and then focus on improving your energies by doing the things you love doing. And throughout the process, stay as centered as you can and divert most of your energies toward yourself and improving your own life; that's when things will really start to gain momentum.

Getting on the right energetic address is even more important than making efforts to get your desire. The Universal postman is the one who is going to be taking most of the action once you place your order; it's the job of the Universe to ensure that the logistics are in place for your desire to reach you. All you have to do is be in a *positive frame of mind* to receive what you've ordered. Worrying about the unavailability of what you want is a surefire way of sending the postman the other way.

Just like you wouldn't call Amazon and constantly inquire about your package after you purchase something from its website, refrain from doing the same with things that you want. Trust that you will receive what you've asked for when your energy levels are the same as your desire.

Your feelings in regard to your desires will always notify you of their proximity to you. Excitement about your desire is an indicator that it will be delivered to you soon. But when you fret about not having it, or wonder how it's going to reach you, that's when this package cannot leave the Universe's warehouse, because you keep *canceling* your desire with your negative thoughts about it.

The harder you try to get to your desire when you are below its level, the more you are going to push it away. There is a balance that needs to be struck to manifest things in your life—the balance of setting out the desire of wanting to experience something (that's the easy part, just like placing an order online) and then getting on the right energetic address where the unavailability of your desire does not bother you. This is the frame of mind with which you can get anything you want.

The Universe's web page isn't powered by the World Wide Web, but with the thoughts that you think. Every time you think a thought about your desire, you are on its corresponding page either placing, tracking, or canceling your order. When you first truly desire something, that's when you place the order. When you feel happy about your desire, you are being notified by the Universe's tracking system that it's on the way. And when you think negative thoughts about your desire, you in effect *cancel* your order.

It's impossible for you to be happy and sad about something at the same time. So, if you cannot muster up the feelings of happiness and excitement while thinking about something you want, just do *not* think about it at all! Think about something else that makes you happy, and look to get on the right energetic address. When your frequencies are high enough, the Universal postman *will find you* and shower you with all that you've asked for and more.

Place your orders

List ten things that you most desire, right now:
1
2
3
4
5
6
7
8
9
10

Get yourself on the right address

List ten activities that can get you in the zone, and temporarily make you *forget* about your desires:

1

2

3

4

5

6

7

8

9

10

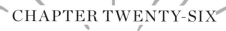

CHAPTER TWENTY-SIX

DATE YOURSELF

Self-love is the *basis* with which a person attracts everything he or she wants. How *worthy* you feel of possessing your desire plays a huge part in it making its way into your experience.

Those who truly love themselves are much better at manifesting the good stuff because they always feel *deserving* of experiencing the desires they hold in their hearts. It's what makes them open to receiving all the things they have asked for.

Deep respect for oneself, however, isn't something a person is born with, but a trait that needs to be inculcated and infused into the very core of one's personality, over time. Those who *practice* self-love are the ones who light up the room every time they enter, and their high regard for themselves reflects in *every* interaction they have with the world around them. These are the ones who are able to ace the manifestation game without even trying.

One of the best ways, then, of practicing the art of self-love, and genuinely looking up to and admiring the person you have become over the years, is by taking *yourself* out on a date every once in a while. By this, I mean actually removing time off your schedule, dressing up, and going to your favorite places by yourself as if you were taking someone else out on a first date.

Bear in mind that this has to be done alone—this date has to be "me time," when *no one else* counts. It doesn't matter if you are in a relationship with the most awesome person in the world; once a week, forget about him or her and everyone else, and take yourself out on a date.

Wear your best clothes, listen to your favorite music, go to a nearby restaurant or any other place you like, and just spend time alone enjoying your own company. When you start having fun hanging out with yourself, others will *also* enjoy spending time with you.

Self-dates are also the best remedy for improving a fractured or a nonexistent love life that so many of us have to put up with these days. Once you start dressing up and going to the places you like, you'll become much more open to attracting a wonderful new relationship or improving an existing one. (Do this for three Sundays in a row, and you'll begin to notice the difference in your interactions with the people you are attracted to—and the way the good things start popping into your life on their own.)

Every other relationship of yours is a reflection of the relationship you have with yourself. Once you work on *deepening* that connection, it will help you get along very well with everyone else as well. Outside influences, and those who seem to have a hold on you, will also start losing their importance in your life as you learn to put yourself at a priority.

Spending high-quality time with yourself will not only help you fall in love with the most important person in your world—you—but will also make you realize that this is the relationship that must come *before* every other relationship.

By pampering and treating yourself, just like you would with the person you love the most, you will not only become extremely comfortable being alone, but your decision-making skills will also improve, and the tendency to act out of fear will diminish. Self-dating will help fill any void that you may be experiencing on an emotional level.

The person you are going to spend the most amount of time with in your life is yourself. Learn to appreciate and value your own company; only then will you find everything else truly enjoyable.

Your ideal date

What would an ideal date look like to you? Fill in the following points about it.

Place:

Time:

Duration:

The clothes you are wearing:

Food you are eating:

The drink in your glass:

Songs you are listening to:

Route you are driving:

Take yourself out on such a date, at least once a month.

Turn your life around

What are the three things you *don't* like about your life, as of today?
1
2
3
Aim to cancel these out in the next three to six months, and watch how the quality of your life becomes *ten* times better than what it currently is.

CHAPTER TWENTY-SEVEN

TAKE A MENTAL HOLIDAY

Going for a vacation is one of those rare events that lends perspective about where we are heading in life, gives us a much-needed break from our routine, prevents a burnout from work, and renews our batteries like few other things can. Taking breaks and getting away from it all not only pumps us up with freshness and enthusiasm but also helps us maintain our sanity.

But with the schedules and deadlines that most of us face these days, it's nearly impossible for us to excuse ourselves from work on a regular basis and go for vacations whenever we feel like, right? And here is where taking a *mental holiday* can make all the difference.

All this process involves is closing your eyes for a few minutes and imagining yourself at your *favorite vacation destination,* picturing yourself immersed in that reality, soaking in that atmosphere, and absorbing all the tranquility and goodness that this place possesses.

You can start by thinking about all the places you've been to in the past that made you feel blissful, and pick the best one of the lot. After you have zeroed in on the place, recollect how you were *feeling* at the time you were there, and do your best to *immerse* yourself in that reality. Become oblivious to what is going around you at the moment, and use this visualization session to go back to that time you felt you were in heaven.

Just like any other visualization process, you'll gain maximum benefit from this immersion if you add as much *richness and detail* as you can to this scene. Make a mental note of everything you see, smell, taste, and touch while you briefly teleport yourself to this destination. Add no agenda to this scene other than wanting to relax and soak in the goodness of your vacation destination. (You can even do this while you are sitting at your desk and taking time off from what you are doing.)

And as you think about your favorite vacation destination often, you'll begin to imbibe the energies of that place and carry those vibes into whatever work you do. Not only will this make you feel better, it will also massively increase your productivity. (Don't be surprised if this little exercise results in you being granted more vacation days once you start vibrating those energies, and your boss notices the improvement in your work.)

The mind is the most powerful organ of the human body; it even has the ability to fool the rest of the body, and our senses, into thinking things that do not reflect the reality surrounding us. Use this to your advantage by habitually conjuring up images that evoke feelings opposite to those that are bogging you down vibrationally.

And since the hectic life that most of us live these days has the ability to get us stressed out, taking a mental holiday will remind you of the fact that **you always have the ability to control the way you** *feel*, **regardless of the pressures or the people that surround you.** You possess the freedom to visualize and experience yourself doing absolutely anything you can think of, and in the process *live* that reality *almost instantly*. That, to me, is the ultimate joy of being human.

Tranquility temples

List ten places you would love to be teleported to:
1
2
3
4
5
6
7
8
9
10

Describe the best place on the previous list, in rich detail:

Name of the place.

What time of the day is it?

What do you see around you?

What is the weather like?

What clothes are you wearing?

What sounds can you hear?

What are you touching with your hands and feet?

CHAPTER TWENTY-EIGHT

KEEP A BACKUP READY

Detachment is the *catalyst* that allows your desires to make their way to you at the fastest speed possible. I know I've said this many times before, but the *only* way of getting and *maintaining* what you want is by reaching a *detached* state of mind, where the manifestation of your desire doesn't really matter to your levels of happiness. This is when you are truly in the vibrational vicinity of the things that you want to experience.

When you are *lighter* about what you want, your desperation no longer causes you to mess things up by taking *more action than what is necessary* to get this desire. Maintaining a healthy distance is the key to unlocking anything that may have previously felt too *large* to make its way into your life.

And apart from religiously removing the time to meditate every day, another great way of achieving this optimum state of detachment is by having something to fall back on if your desire doesn't manifest as quickly as you want it to.

Having a proper, good old-fashioned "backup plan" is what allows you to reach the ideal vantage point from which you are able to see the best way of bringing about the *original* desire into your experience.

When you have something to fall back on, not only does your subconscious barrier of the fear of being rejected reduce, but you also become more open to receiving your original desire because its energies no longer feel alien to you. Paradoxically, the backup is what almost guarantees the manifestation of your first desire, should you wish to experience it.

The sweet spot from which you can manifest anything you want is when you *want* something to happen, but do *not need* it to happen, for you to feel better. This is a state in which your desire feels purer because you genuinely want to experience it for the happiness that you are going to get out of it, not because it is going to fill a void that you may be experiencing in your life.

You also stop acting needy and desperate once you know that there is always something else that will give you similar amounts of happiness. This makes you take just the right amount of action to get to your desire.

Trying to force something to happen, by doing *more* to get it than what feels good, is an indication that your vibrations have been kinked by desperation; it's when your need to *take happiness* from your desire supersedes the happiness that you want to give to it. Taking more action than what is necessary is one the biggest reasons that desires do not manifest.

So, **to overcome this very human tendency of acting out of desperation to get something you don't possess but *really* desire, learn to cultivate as many options as you can.** Date multiple people until you get married, do a second job that you love on the weekends, have at least two sources of income, diversify your investments, have multiple sets of friends, take insurance for your health and property, develop as many hobbies as you possibly can, and *always* keep a backup ready.

By not putting all your hopes on *one* outcome, it becomes easier for the Universe to guide you down the path of least resistance, by gradually directing you toward the best option of the lot, in the easiest way possible.

If you obsess about your desire, you sort of miss the point of feeling good about experiencing it. But when you keep your options open, not only does the obsessiveness dissolve, but there is also a sense of easiness that fills you up from inside, as you rest in the knowledge that even if one particular desire takes quite awhile to manifest, things are going to be just fine.

The backup plans

List your top ten desires, and what you would do if they didn't manifest as quickly as you want them to:	
Desire	**Backup**
1	
2	
3	
4	
5	
6	
7	
8	
9	
10	

Your fallback options

List three things you could do on the weekends to supplement your income:
1
2
3
List three people you could date if your girlfriend/boyfriend decided to go their own way:
1
2
3
List three friends that could replace your best friend if he/she were to leave town:
1
2
3
List three health insurance plans that could provide cover for you in the event of a prolonged illness:
1
2
3

CHAPTER TWENTY-NINE

REFUSE TO PLAY THE GAME

We seem to have a conscious say in very little of the world we find ourselves in. Being born into an environment that was shaped by others, having uncountable rules thrust upon us, or inheriting the genetic structure of people who happen to be our parents, doesn't exactly seem like a scenario of our choosing. Come to think of it, we really aren't that different from avatars in a highly complex video game.

Yet, most of us drudgingly press on with our lives, not realizing the fact that we have the power to slowly start *shaping* this game and the circumstances that surround us in accordance with our wishes and needs. We have the ability to make this simulation whatever we want it to be, and the capabilities to make our avatar one of the best players around. Everything we can imagine ourselves experiencing in this human form is possible for us to create.

But for that, we need to start looking at *everything* as if we *were* playing a game, and not get so caught up in our everyday "reality." We just need to make that *shift* in the way we perceive things and be *light* about it all; that's when things can really start changing. And guess what? There are indicators, too, that let you know how well your avatar is doing.

There are *three* major variables/scores that give a good indication of your performance here on planet Earth—your health, the quality of your interpersonal relationships, and the amount of money you possess. If you have these three in abundance, you pretty much have it *all* and are at the top of your game.

If, like most of the others, it doesn't quite feel like you're there yet, the aim of your avatar should be to *maximize* these three variables to live a high-quality life. The level of happiness (*or lack of it*) that you experience in these areas will give you a fair idea of how well you seem to be doing. The happier you *feel* about any of those three aspects of your life, the better the game gets.

And one of the best ways of boosting up your score in *each* of those areas, and gaining invaluable insights on how to better proceed with your life, is by creating a *distance* between yourself and your current reality, by taking a day off to do *absolutely nothing.* That is, **one day each month, not living the life that the world demands you live, and simply existing.**

On this day, money, friends, lovers, health, entertainment, or anything else, for that matter, have to be forgotten, and you need to just *watch* the whole thing like a gamer taking a pizza break would watch his avatar stand still in a video game.

This simple act of taking mindful time off, and not getting so caught up with your life, will give you ideas that would have otherwise skipped your attention because of how *immersed* you were in your reality.

You could practice this process for a few hours to begin with and then slowly extend it to an entire Sunday. And as you start doing it more frequently, you will eventually reach a stage where you will clearly be able to see what is going on around you, and be able to figure out ways to improve the areas of your life that you find less than ideal.

Tell your family and friends that you will be requiring some time to yourself, and find a place where you can be alone. Forget about everything else and just be with yourself. Do not read or watch anything; just *exist*. As hard as you may find it initially, the payoff in terms of your ability to sustain periods of peace will be well worth it in the end.

Apart from giving you the much-needed break that you deserve from playing this complex game that is your *life,* and the ever-evolving character that is *you*, this exercise will also give your avatar the chance to recharge his or her batteries and have a better shot at winning than ever before.

The most important variables

What would you like your life to be like in six months, in the following three aspects? Write up to three quantifiable manifestations in each.		
Finances	Health	Interpersonal Relationships
1		
2		
3		
Look at the table the night before you practice this process of taking a break.		

Your silent zones

Find out and list ten places that will allow you to be by yourself:
1
2
3
4
5
6
7
8
9
10

CHAPTER THIRTY

PRACTICE LAST-DAY LIVING

Last but definitely not least, to master the manifestation game, you *have* to start living your life to the *fullest*; only this way will you attain the energy to manifest the things that have perpetually seemed beyond your reach. Magic happens when you are vibrating at the highest frequencies accessible to you at any moment.

And **a surefire way of reaching your highest possible vibration is by asking yourself, "If this were my last day or last few hours here on Earth, what would I be doing?,"** and then following the impulse that *first* comes to your head.

This impulse could lead you to do something unrelated to what you want, it could make you look at your desires in a completely new way, or it could cause you to do something you've never done before; all of which will help in achieving those stellar energies required to manifest your biggest desires.

Living each day as if it were your last is by far the *most* exciting way to live and can add the extra zing to everything you do. Once you consciously start living this way, you will rendezvous with people, circumstances, and opportunities that would've otherwise seemed elusive, rendezvous that will help you move toward the life of your dreams in the fastest way possible.

You will *feel* the energy move through you when you follow this process, and all tiredness will escape the body when your brain is not burdened by wanting to please others or trying to do things for an imaginary future. Even people around you will appreciate the increased enthusiasm that will accompany you everywhere you go.

This way of living essentially means that you no longer live as the identity that you have carved out for yourself over the years, but rather, you will unite with your soul and live without any baggage from the past or worry of the future, resulting in one of the most liberating periods of your life experience.

Only when you are true to yourself and make it a point to go after your immediate desires, on a consistent basis, do you find your highest joy and, eventually, the life of your dreams. And last-day living is what will take you closest to your true, joyous, expansive, and *excited* self.

At any moment, if you feel low, look at the clock and remind yourself that these might be the last few hours of your life. Remind yourself that you don't need anyone's approval to have fun or do the things you've always wanted to do. And then go ahead and please yourself in *any* way that you deem fit.

And at the end of every day, look back and recollect the things you did that were *worthy* of being classified as something that you would've done on your last day (aim to do at least three to five such activities daily). There really shouldn't be any other way of living your life. Things that don't fall into the last-day category are just bull$%#@ that has been imposed on you by society.

On the days or other time periods you consciously decide to follow this process, make sure you choose your heart over your mind at all times. There might be instances where you feel you *must* or *should* do something; learn to ignore your brain and follow your gut and do the things you *want* to be doing instead. Following your instincts and being true to yourself are what will maintain the purity and power of the process.

Last-day living is just like any other art form; the more you practice it, the better you will become at it and at following your highest excitement—and the higher your vibrations will be. At first, doing things you really *want* to be doing might feel alien to you because of how much you've been listening to everyone else but yourself. But with practice, you will get better and better at following your inner voice and chasing your *highest* excitement, both of which will rapidly lead you to the joyous path you are meant to be on.

The last-day stuff

If it were your last day on Earth, what are some of the things you'd be doing?

Who would you be spending most of your time with? (It's okay even if you write your own name.)

What type of clothes would you be wearing?

What would you be eating/drinking?

How "last-day" is your life?

Which of these daily activities of yours fit the last-day criteria? (Circle the appropriate ones)
The work you do
The friends you hang out with
The amount of exercise you get
The amount of time you spend with the people you love
The amount of time you spend outdoors
The amount of time you spend with yourself
The clothes you wear
The songs you listen to
The challenges you take on
The places you spend most of your time in
The amount of self-love you practice

CONCLUSION

If you had to take one thing from this book, let it be that manifestation is an inside job. First change your state of being, and then your entire life changes to reflect what is going on within you.

Getting the things you want is *really* a feelings game; the better you feel, the better your life becomes. And every technique in this book is designed to make you feel good—making you more and more receptive to your desires.

So my final advice to you is to do whatever it takes to be *happy*. The Universe will take care of everything else beautifully. It is Law.

RESOURCES

Chopra, Deepak. *The Seven Spiritual Laws of Success*. San Rafael, CA: Amber-Allen, 1994.

Ferriss, Timothy. *The 4-Hour Work Week*. London: Vermilion Books, 2008.

Hendricks, Gay. *The Big Leap*. New York: HarperCollins, 2009.

Hicks, Esther, and Jerry Hicks. *The Law of Attraction*. Carlsbad, CA: Hay House, 2006.

Murphy, Joseph. *The Power of Your Subconscious Mind*. Mumbai: Embassy Books, 2010.

Samuels, Michael. *Keep Calm and Ask On*. New York: CreateSpace, 2014.

APPENDIX

Each of the activities mentioned in chapter 3 is very powerful in its own right and has a direct correlation with what most of us would want to manifest.

Sun/Moon

Watching the sunrise is correlated with the level of our earnings. Increase the number of sunrises you see in the year, and your earnings are bound to grow.

This is because, on a subconscious level, a sunrise signifies potential. The only reason your finances aren't what you want them to be is because you are not living to your potential. Each sunrise brings with it the promise and potential of a brand-new day for you to turn your life around.

Getting up early and seeing the sunrise means that you are ready for the day, that you've gotten a head start, and that you are a step ahead of the others. A lot of studies have reported that people who "beat the sun to the starting line" on a regular basis go on to do very well for themselves financially and professionally.

Waking up early also gives you clarity of thought and makes it very easy to hear your inner GPS. You have time to gather your thoughts, reflect on where you are heading in life, and decide on the best course of action for that particular day.

Watching the sunset is correlated with the quality of your intimate relationships.

Subconsciously, the setting sun makes you realize that everything will end one day. Deep down, you know that even though you may have spent years with a person you love, the relationship will end at some point (either through one person passing over, or because your paths diverge). This makes you less prone to negativity toward the people you love.

Watching the sunset makes you wiser, calmer, and more contemplative. And each time you do this activity, your intimate relationships will get stronger, bringing with them rich rewards of the feelings of security and love.

The amount of sunlight you get has an impact on your finances, since this energy is the epitome of nature's abundance. Only a fraction of the sun's light reaches the Earth, and yet it is enough to sustain all life on this planet—that's how powerful, abundant, and unfathomably large this energy is. And since most of us associate abundance with money, soaking in the sun's energy is bound to have an impact on the material abundance in our lives as well.

Gazing at the moon is correlated with your ability to get along with difficult people, coworkers, or relatives, and the ability to stay calm in tough situations.

This activity instills a sense of peace in you, and on a subconscious level, it allows you see the beauty in other people's flaws, just like you see the beauty in the moon despite all the dark patches that cover its surface.

Looking at the full moon can also help you control your temper. (The moon is considered to be the antithesis of the fiery sun, and its personality is considered to be cool, calm, and composed.)

Animals/Plants

Feeding an animal is correlated with compassion and your ability to get along with people who are not as smart as you are.

Some of us are afflicted with a superiority complex that makes it difficult for us to get along with people we consider less intelligent than us; in fact, we are quite often driven up the wall by some of them.

But everyone has something to offer to you and something to bring to the table, which you may not have thought of otherwise. Nature always gifts each and everyone with unique strengths; we just don't realize it.

Feeding an animal will definitely help you get along with people who are not as smart as you, and in return, they will help you in ways that only they possibly can. I recommend all employers to do this activity on a regular basis. This small act of kindness and connecting with nature will help you bring out the best in your workers and improve your relationship with your employees, which, in turn, will increase their morale and, eventually, the profits of your organization.

Watering a plant is correlated with nurturing and patience. This is one of the activities that will improve your relationships with people who are younger than you.

If you have kids you are finding difficult to control, this activity will help increase your patience with them and with your desires in general.

Subconsciously, you will understand that just like you cannot expect a plant to spring forth flowers a day after you've watered it, you must not lose your cool if your desire doesn't manifest immediately. Rest assured that if you "water" your desires by thinking about them in a positive and expectant way, they will eventually manifest.

And this sense of "looking after a plant" will spill into other aspects of your life as well and improve your relationship with kids. You'll find yourself being a better and calmer mentor to them.

Food

Cooking your meals is correlated with your overall health, maintaining your ideal weight, and security.

If you are suffering from ill health of any kind, make it a point to cook at least one meal for yourself, every day, and enjoy eating it. When you know that a meal is going to be ingested by you, you are naturally going to put more love and care into the process, and this energy is going to flow right into your body.

I learned at a very young age that the energy that food is made with has as big an impact on health and how the nutrients in the food express themselves. This is why fast food has low energy, because the person making/assembling it is almost always doing it to get it over with, and food made for a special occasion (e.g., Christmas, Thanksgiving, Diwali, or Eid) has high energy.

On a subconscious level, this activity lets you know that you are taking care of yourself and will be able to fend for yourself when the time comes; this gives you a sense of security and pride.

Walking

Going for a walk by yourself helps you connect with your inner GPS like nothing else can; this activity always gives you insights on the best course to take.

The insights you get from taking a walk by yourself will help you make better decisions, and you'll find yourself making fewer and fewer mistakes as a result. This activity will also help you choose the best course of action when you are faced with a choice, and your life will grow more expansive as a result.

When you are out walking with a friend, it will take your bond with them to another level. The conversations will generally be upbeat, you'll find yourself walking more than you otherwise would have, and the combined perspective will give you more ideas on how to improve your life. This activity is probably the best therapy there is.

Cold Baths

The number of cold baths you take is correlated with your health, immunity, and ability to meet new people and start new ventures.

Several studies have linked cold baths to increased immunity and better health. People who take cold baths are much less likely to get the flu and common cold. Taking cold showers can also ward off depression; it keeps your hair healthy, increases testosterone and fertility, and improves circulation of blood in the body.

Subconsciously, taking cold baths makes you believe that you can take on tough times with ease, and adds resilience to your character. It also means that you are willing to get out of your comfort zone more often; this is what allows you to easily make new friends, make new business associates, and meet new people at parties. Cold baths also increase your chances of finding romance (since we always have to get out of our comfort zone to meet someone new).

We are so used to our warm baths that this activity is probably the toughest thing to do on this list. You can start by gradually reducing the temperature of your bath and then eventually removing heat from it altogether. I'm saying this only because it's the natural way of living, and this is how our ancestors lived; it's also how our bodies are designed (to be cleansed with cold water).

Exercise/Sports

The number of outdoor activities is correlated with the quality and quantity of your friendships and social connections, and the ability to start new business ventures.

Most outdoor activities involve other people, coordination, and teamwork of some sort. It is very hard for you to be selfish while performing these activities, and this helps you build your relationships and friendships.

These activities teach you how to get along with people who may not be as talented as you are, and to match up to people who are much better at the sport. Regardless of whom you are playing with, you always gain something in terms of understanding people.

Outdoor activities also help ward off depression, they help keep the negative thoughts at bay, and they are the most fun and high-vibrational activities that human beings can possibly think of doing. They also bring out the competitive instincts within us, which helps us in other aspects of our lives as well.

Perform at least one outdoor activity a week and see the drastic improvement in your manifestations.

Summary

I suggest you make a note of the number of times you do all of these activities, in your calendar. Then, look at year-end results by comparing the number of times you did these activities with your manifestations.

For example, compare the number of meals you have cooked for yourself in a particular year with the weight that you managed to lose (if that's what you want), or with the number of days you fell sick with a stomach infection or flu. Compare the number of cold baths you took with the number of new friends that you made in that particular year. Look at the total against sunrises watched and compare it with the balance in your bank account each year. You'll be able to spot clear correlations with the aspects of your life that have been mentioned.

Feel free to add more natural activities you can think of, and compare them with major indicators of the quality of your life, such as income, number of friends, number of parties attended/hosted, body fat percentage, etc.

Measuring is the key to quantifying and realizing the drastic effect these natural activities have on our well-being. Peter Drucker famously said, "You can't manage what you can't measure." Measuring the impact that Nature has on your manifestations is one of the few ways of quantifying its vibration.

You'll be out of your house more often once you realize the effect that Nature is having on your life.

MISHAL KARAMCHANDANI has been a professor of economics for the past eight years. After completing his postgraduation at Lancaster University, Mishal came back to Mumbai to pursue a fulfilling and rewarding teaching career that also allowed him to explore his other interests, including theater, music, and writing. The Law of Attraction (LOA) has fascinated him since he was a teenager. Noticing that most LOA books rarely offer practical advice, Mishal decided to write *The Book of Manifestations* to help people use the Law on an everyday basis.